ILLUSTRATIVE NOTES ON

THE PILGRIM'S PROGRESS

KNOCK
& IT SHALL BE OPENED UNTO YOU

MERCY AT THE WICKET GATE

ILLUSTRATIVE NOTES ON

THE PILGRIM'S PROGRESS

BY

REV. THOMAS SCOTT

COMPILED BY
CHARLES J. DOE

CURIOSMITH
MINNEAPOLIS
2011

Published by Curiosmith.
P. O. Box 390293, Minneapolis, Minnesota, 55439.
Internet: curiosmith.com.
E-mail: shopkeeper@curiosmith.com.

Previously published in separate numbers by J. Parsons
during the years 1794–1795.

ISBN 9781935626398

CONTENTS

PREFACE

THE high estimation, in which the PILGRIM'S PROGRESS has been held for much above a century, sufficiently evinces its intrinsic value: and there is every reason to suppose, that it will be read with admiration and advantage for ages to come, probably till the consummation of all things.

The pious Christian, in proportion to "his growth in grace, and in the knowledge of Jesus Christ," derives more and more instruction from repeated perusals of this remarkable book; while his enlarged experience and extended observation enable him to unfold, with progressive evidence, the meaning of the agreeable similitudes employed by its ingenious author: and even the careless reader is fascinated to attention, by the simple and artless manner in which the interesting narrative is arranged. Nor should this be represented as mere amusement, for it has been observed, by men of great discernment and acquaintance with the human mind, that young persons, having perused the PILGRIM as a pleasing tale, often retain a remembrance of its leading incidents, which, after continuing perhaps in a dormant state for several years, has at length germinated, as it were, into the most important and seasonable instruction; while the events of their own lives placed it before their minds in a new and affecting point of view. It may, therefore, be questioned, whether modern ages have produced any work which has more promoted the best interests of mankind.

These observations indeed more especially apply to the First Part of the PILGRIM'S PROGRESS; as *that* is complete in itself, and in all respects superior to the Second. Yet *this* also contains many edifying and interesting passages: though, in unity of design, in arrangement of incident, and in simplicity of allegory, it is not comparable to the other. Indeed the author, in his first effort, had nearly exhausted his subject; and nothing remained for his second attempt, but a few detached episodes to his original design: nor could any vigor of genius have wrought them up to an equal degree of interest. It must, however, be allowed, that Mr. Bunyan here, in some instances, sinks below himself, both in fertility of invention, force of imagination, and aptness of illustration; nay, he occasionally stoops to a puerile play of fancy, and a refined nicety in doctrine, which do not well accord to the rest of the work. Yet the same grand principles of evangelical and practical religion, which stamp an inestimable value on the First Part, are in the Second also exhibited with equal purity, though not with equal simplicity: and, on many occasions, the author rises superior to his disadvantages; and introduces characters and incidents, which arrest the attention, and deeply interest the heart, of every pious and intelligent reader.

It would not perhaps be difficult to prove, that the PILGRIM'S PROGRESS is as really an original production of vigorous native genius, as any of those works, in prose or verse, which have excited the admiration of mankind, through successive ages and in different nations. It does not indeed possess those ornaments which are often mistaken for intrinsic excellence; but the rudeness of its style (which at the same time is aptly characteristic of the subject) concurs to prove it a most extraordinary book: for, had it not been written with very great ingenuity, a religious treatise, evidently inculcating doctrines always offensive, but now more unfashionable than formerly, could not, in so homely a garb, have durably attracted the attention of a polished age and nation. Yet it is undeniable, that BUNYAN's PILGRIM continues to be read and admired by vast multitudes; while publications on a similar plan, by persons of respectable learning and talents, are consigned to almost total neglect and oblivion.

This is not, however, that view of the work, which entitles it to its highest honor, or most endears it to the pious mind: for, comparing it with the other productions of the same author, (which are indeed edifying to the humble believer, but not much suited to the taste of the ingenious) we shall be led to conclude, that in penning this, he was favored with a peculiar measure of divine assistance: especially when we recollect, that, within the confines of a jail, he was able so to delineate the Christian's course, with its various difficulties, perils, conflicts, and supports, that scarcely any thing seems to have escaped his notice. Indeed, the accurate observer of the church in his own days, and the learned student of ecclesiastical history, must be equally surprised to find, that hardly one remarkable character, good or bad, or mixed in any manner or proportion imaginable; or one fatal delusion, by-path, or injurious mistake, can be singled out, which may not be paralleled in the PILGRIM'S PROGRESS; that is, as to the grand outlines; for the *minutia*, about which bigoted and frivolous minds waste their zeal and force, are, with very few exceptions, wisely passed over. This circumstance is not only very surprising, but it suggests an argument, perhaps unanswerable, in confirmation of the divine authority of those religious sentiments, which are now often derided under the title of *orthodoxy*. For every part of this singular book *exclusively* suits the different descriptions of such as profess those doctrines; and relates the experiences, mistakes, falls, recoveries, distresses, temptations, and consolations of serious persons of this class in our own times, as exactly as if it had been penned from the observation of them, and for their immediate benefit; while, like the sacred Scriptures, it remains a sealed book to all who are strangers to evangelical religion.

These remarks may very properly be concluded with the words of a justly admired poet of the present day, who in the following lines has fully sanctioned all that has been here advanced—

> 'O thou, whom, borne on fancy's eager wing
> Back to the seasons of life's happy spring,
> I pleas'd remember, and while mem'ry yet,
> Holds fast her office here, can ne'er forget;
> Ingenious dreamer, in whose well told tale
> Sweet fiction and sweet truth alike prevail;
> Whose hum'rous vein, strong sense, and simple style,
> May teach the gayest, make the gravest smile;
> Witty, and well employ'd, and, like thy Lord,
> Speaking in parables his slighted word;
> I name thee not, lest so despis'd a name
> Should move a sneer at thy deserved fame;
> Yet e'en in transitory life's late day,
> That mingles all my brown with sober grey,

Revere the man, whose PILGRIM marks the road
And guides the PROGRESS of the soul to God.
'Twere well with most if books, that could engage
Their childhood, pleas'd them at a riper age;
The man approving what had charm'd the boy,
Would die at last in comfort, peace, and joy,
And not with curses on his art who stole
The gem of truth from his unguarded soul.'

COWPER, TIROCINIUM, V. 129.

[THE FOLLOWING PREFACE WAS INCLUDED IN SOME EARLY EDITIONS.]

SEVERAL persons have already favored the public with original explanatory notes, of the nature of those here published; but the editor, on mature deliberation, did not think himself precluded by this consideration, from communicating his sentiments on a favorite book, according to a plan he had formed in his own mind. Every man who thinks for himself has his own views of a subject, which often vary, more or less, from the sentiments of others, whom he nevertheless esteems and loves with great cordiality: and the great Head of the Church has entrusted different talents to his servants, to qualify them for usefulness among distinct descriptions of persons. It is indeed incontrovertible, that some men will receive the great truths of Christianity with candor and docility, when exhibited in a style and manner suited to their peculiar taste, who disregard and reject them, when conveyed in language which numbers, perhaps justly, think far more interesting and affecting. It need not, therefore, be apprehended, that the labors of different writers on the same subject should materially interfere with each other: rather we may indulge an hope, that, as far as they accord to the standard of divine truth, they will, in different circles, promote the common cause of vital godliness.

The editor's aim, in this attempt to elucidate the PILGRIM'S PROGRESS, is, to give a brief key to the grand outlines of the allegory, from which the attentive reader may obtain a general idea of the author's design;—to bestow more pains in fixing the precise meaning of those parts, which might most perplex the inquirer, and which seem to have most escaped notice, or divided the sentiments, of expositors;—to state and establish, compendiously but clearly, those doctrinal, practical, and experimental views of Christianity, which Mr. Bunyan meant to convey; to guard them carefully from those extremes and perversions which he never favored, but which too frequently increase men's prejudices against them; to delineate the more prominent features of his various characters, with a special reference to the present state of religious profession, distinguishing accurately what he approves, from the defects even of true Pilgrims;—and in fine, to give as just a representation, as may be, of the author's sentiments concerning the right way to heaven, and of the many false ways and by-paths, which prove injurious to all who venture into them, and fatal to unnumbered multitudes. In executing this plan, no information that the editor could procure has been neglected; but he does not invariably adhere to the sentiments of any man: and while his dependence is placed, as he hopes, on the promised teaching of the Holy Spirit, he does not think himself authorized to spare any pains, in endeavoring to render the publication acceptable and useful.

The text is printed, as it stands in the oldest editions, which may be supposed to contain the author's own terms, which later editors have frequently modernized. A few obsolete or unclassical words, and unusual phrases, seem to become the character of the Pilgrim; and they are often more emphatical than any which can be substituted in their stead. Some exceptions, however, have been admitted; as the author, if living, would probably change a very few expressions for such as are less offensive to modem ears; and in other instances the slips of his pen, while taken up with things of vastly superior importance, would now be mistaken for errors of the press. Great pains have been taken to collate different copies of the work, and to examine every scriptural reference; in order to render this edition, in all respects, as correct as possible.—The editor has the satisfaction of adding, that he has been favored by Mrs. Gurney, Holborn, with the use of the second edition of the First Part of the PILGRIM, by which he has been enabled to correct many errors of subsequent editions. The author's *marginal references* seemed so essential a part of the work, that it was deemed indispensably requisite to insert them in their places. But as the *marginal notes* do not appear to convey any material instruction distinct from that contained in the text, and to be principally useful in pointing out any passage, to which the reader might wish to refer; it was thought most advisable to omit them, and to supply their place by a *running title* on the top of every page, conveying as nearly as possible the same ideas: for, indeed, they so incumber the page, and break in upon the uniformity of printing, that all hope of elegance must be precluded while they are regained.

Mr. Bunyan prefaced each part of the PILGRIM'S PROGRESS with a copy of verses: but as his poetry does not suit the taste of these days, and is by no means equal to the work itself, it hath been deemed expedient to omit them. That prefixed to the First Part is entitled 'The Author's Apology for his Book;' in which he informs the reader that he was unawares drawn into the allegory, when employed about another work; that the further he proceeded, the more rapidly did ideas flow into his mind; and this induced him to form it into a separate book; and that, showing it to his friends—

'Some said, "John, print it," others said, "Not so;"
Some said, "It might do good;" others said, "No."'

The public will not hesitate in determining which opinion was the result of the deeper penetration; but will wonder that a long apology for so valuable a publication should have been deemed necessary. This was, however, the case; and the author, having solidly, though rather verbosely, answered several objections and adduced some obvious arguments in very unpoetical rhymes, concludes with these lines, which may serve as a favorable specimen of the whole.—

'Would'st thou divert thyself from melancholy?
Would'st thou be pleasant, yet be far from folly?
Would'st thou read riddles and their explanation?
Or else be drowned in thy contemplation?
Dost thou love picking meat? Or would'st thou see
A man i' th' clouds, and hear him speak to thee?
Would'st thou be in a dream, and yet not sleep?
Or would'st thou in a moment laugh and weep?
Or would'st thou lose thyself, and catch no harm?
And find thyself again without a charm?
Would'st read thyself, and read thou know'st not what,
And yet know whether thou art blest or not,
By reading the same lines? O then come hither,
And lay my book, thy heart and head together.'

The poem prefixed to the Second Part, in a kind of dialogue between the author and his book, is still less interesting; and serves to show, that he had a more favorable opinion of its comparative merit, than posterity has formed; which is no singular case.—Some verses are likewise found at the bottom of certain plates that accompanied several of the old editions, which they, who omit the plates, or substitute others, know not where to insert. To show all regard, however, to every thing that Mr. BUNYAN wrote, *as a part of the work*, they will be found in the notes on the incidents to which they refer.

THE LIFE

OF

JOHN BUNYAN

THE celebrated author of the PILGRIM'S PROGRESS was born, A.D. 1628, at ELSTOW, a small village near BEDFORD. His father earned his bread by the low occupation of a tinker; but he bore a fair character, and took care that his son, whom he brought up to the same business, should be taught to read and write. We are told, indeed, that he quickly forgot all he had learned, through his extreme profligacy: yet it is probable, that he retained so much as enabled him to recover the rest, when his mind became better disposed; and that it was very useful to him in the subsequent part of his life.

The materials, from which an account of this valuable man must be compiled, are so scanty and imperfect, that nothing very satisfactory must be expected. He seems from his earliest youth to have been greatly addicted to gross vice as well as impiety: yet he was interrupted in his course by continual alarms and convictions, which were sometimes peculiarly overwhelming; but they had no other effect at the time, than to extort from him the most absurd wishes that can be imagined. A copious narrative of these early conflicts and crimes is contained in a treatise published by himself, under the title of *Grace abounding to the chief of Sinners.*

During this part of his life he was twice preserved from the most imminent danger of drowning: and being a soldier in the parliament's army at the siege of Leicester, A.D. 1645, he was drawn out to stand sentinel; but one of his comrades, having by his own desire taken his place, was shot through the head on his post; and thus BUNYAN was reserved by the all-disposing hand of GOD for better purposes. He seems, however, to have made progressive advances in wickedness, and to have become the ring-leader of youth in every kind of profaneness and excess.

His career of vice received a considerable check, in consequence of his marriage with the daughter of a person who had been very religious in his way, and remarkably bold in reproving vice, but who was then dead. His wife's discourse to him concerning her father's piety, excited him to go regularly to church: and as she brought him, for her whole portion, *The Practice of Piety*, and *The plain Man's Path-way to Heaven*, he employed himself frequently in reading these books.

The events recorded of our author are so destitute of dates, and regard to the order in which they happened, that no clear arrangement can now be made of them: but it is probable that this new attention to religion, though ineffectual to the reformation of his conduct, rendered him more susceptible of convictions; and his vigorous imagination, at that time altogether untutored by knowledge or discretion, laid him open to a variety of impressions, sleeping and waking, which he verily supposed to arise from words spoken to him, or objects presented before his bodily senses; and he never after was able to break the association of ideas which was thus formed in his mind. Accordingly he says, that one day when he was engaged in diversion with his companions, 'A voice did suddenly dart from heaven into my soul, which said, *Wilt thou leave thy sins and go to heaven, or have thy sins and go to hell?*' The consciousness of his wicked course of life, accompanied with the recollection of the truths he had read, suddenly meeting in his mind, thus produced a violent alarm, and made such an impression on his imagination, that he seemed to have heard these words, and to have seen CHRIST frowning and menacing him. But we must not suppose, that there was any miracle wrought; nor could there be any occasion for a new revelation to suggest or enforce so scriptural a warning. This may serve as a specimen of those *impressions,* which constitute a large part of his religious experience, but which it is not advisable to recapitulate.

He was next tempted to conclude that it was then too late to repent or seek salvation; and, as he ignorantly listened to the suggestion, he indulged his corrupt inclinations without restraint, imagining that this was the only way in which he could possibly have the least expectation of pleasure, during his whole existence.

While he was proceeding in this wretched course, a woman of very bad character reproved him with great severity for profane swearing; declaring in the strongest expressions, that he exceeded in it all men she had ever heard. This made him greatly ashamed, when he reflected that he was too vile even for such a bad woman to endure: so that from that time he began to break off that odious custom.—His guilty and terrified mind was also prepared to admit the most alarming impressions during his sleep: and he had such a dream about the day of judgment, and its awful circumstances and consequences, as powerfully influenced his conduct. There was, indeed, nothing very extraordinary in this; for such dreams are not uncommon to men under deep convictions: yet the LORD was doubtless, by all these means, secretly influencing his heart, and warning him to flee from the wrath to come.

He was, however, reluctant to part with his irreligious associates and vain pleasures; till the conversation of a poor man, who came in his way, induced him to read the Bible, especially the preceptive and historical parts of it: and this put him upon an entire reformation of his conduct; so that his neighbors were greatly astonished at the change. In this manner he went on for about a year; at some times satisfied with himself, and at others distressed with fears and consciousness of guilt. Indeed, he seems ever after to have considered all these convictions and desires as wholly originating from natural principles; but in this perhaps some persons will venture to dissent from him. A self-righteous dependence accompanied with self-complacency, and furnishing incentives to pride, is indeed a full proof of unregeneracy: but conscientiousness connected with disquietudes, humiliation for sin, and a disposition to wait for divine teaching, is an effect and evidence of *life*, though the mind be yet darkened with ignorance, error, and prejudice. And he, that hath given life will give it more abundantly; for, "The path of the just is as the shining light, that shineth more and more unto the perfect day."

While BUNYAN was in this state of mind he went to BEDFORD, in the exercise of his trade as a tinker, where he overheard some women discourse about regeneration: and though he did not understand their meaning, he was greatly affected by observing the earnestness, cheerfulness, and humility of their behavior; and he was also convinced that his own views of religion were very defective. Being thus led to frequent their company, he was brought as it were into a new world. Such an entire change took place in his views and affections, and his mind was so deeply engaged in contemplating the great concerns of eternity, and the things pertaining to the kingdom of GOD, that he found it very difficult to employ his thoughts on any secular affairs.

But this extraordinary flow of affections, not being attended by doctrinal information in any measure proportionable, laid him open to various attempts of Satan and his emissaries. The RANTERS, a set of the vilest antinomians that almost ever existed, first assailed him by one of their party, who had formerly been Mr. BUNYAN's companion in vice: but he over-acted his part; and, proceeding even to deny the being of a GOD, probably furnished the character of ATHEIST in the PILGRIM'S PROGRESS. While Mr. BUNYAN was engaged in reading the books of the RANTERS, not being able to form his judgment about them, he was led to offer up the following prayer: 'O Lord, I am a fool, and not able to know the truth from error: Lord, leave me not to my own blindness, either to approve or condemn this doctrine. If it be of GOD, let me not despise it; if it be of the devil, let me not embrace it. Lord, I lay my soul in this matter only at thy foot; let me not be deceived, I humbly beseech thee.' No experienced Christian will be surprised to find, that the Lord, in an evident manner, graciously answered this most suitable request. Mr. BUNYAN soon saw through the delusions of the RANTERS; and probably referred to them, under the character of SELF-WILL, in the second part of this work.

The Epistles of ST. PAUL, which he now read with great attention, but without any guide or instructor, gave occasion to his being assaulted by many sore temptations. He found the apostle continually speaking of *faith;* and he could not understand the meaning of that word, or discover whether he was a believer or not; so that, mistaking the words of CHRIST,[1] he was tempted to seek a solution of this difficulty by trying to work a miracle. He thought however it would be right to pray, before he made the attempt, and thus he was induced to desist, though his difficulties still remained. On another occasion he was delivered from great perplexities about the doctrine of election, by reflecting that none "ever trusted in GOD and was

1 Matthew 17:20.

confounded;" and therefore it would be best for him to trust in
GOD, and leave election, as a "secret thing," with the Lord to
whom it belonged. And the general invitations of the gospel,
and the assurance that "yet there is room," helped him to repel
the temptation to conclude that the day of grace was past.

This brief account of his temptations and escapes may teach
others the best way of resisting similar suggestions: and it may
show us, that numbers are durably harassed by such perplexities, for want of doctrinal knowledge and faithful instructors
and counsellors. He was, however, afterwards enabled, by
means of these inward trials, to caution others to better effect
and more tenderly to sympathize with the tempted.

After some time Mr. BUNYAN became acquainted with Mr.
GIFFORD, an Antipoedo-baptist minister at BEDFORD, whose conversation was very useful to him: yet he was in some respects
more discouraged than ever, by fuller discoveries of those evils
in his heart, which he had not before noticed; and by doubts concerning the truth of the Scriptures, which his entire ignorance of
the evidences by which they are most completely authenticated,
rendered durably perplexing to him. He was, however, at length
relieved by a sermon he heard on the love of CHRIST; though
the grounds, on which he derived satisfaction and encouragement from it, are not very accurately stated. Soon after this he
was admitted, by adult baptism, a member of Mr. GIFFORD's
church, A.D. 1655, being then twenty-seven years of age; and
after a little time, he was earnestly desired by the congregation
to expound or preach, in a manner which is customary among
the Dissenters, as a preparation to the ministry. For a while he
resisted their importunity, under a deep sense of his incompe-
tency; but at length he was prevailed upon to speak in a small
company, which he did greatly to their satisfaction and edification. Having been thus proved for a considerable time, he was
at length called forth, and set apart by fasting and prayer to
the ministerial office, which he executed with faithfulness and
success during a long course of years; though frequently with
the greatest trepidation and inward disquietude.

As he was baptized 1655, and imprisoned 1660, he could
not have been long engaged in the work when the latter event
took place: and it does not appear whether he obtained a stated
employment as a minister; or whether he only preached occasionally, and continued to work at his trade; as many Dissenters

very laudably do, when called to minister among poor people, that they "may not be burdensome to them." Previously however to the restoration of CHARLES II, when the churches were principally filled by those who have since been distinguished as non-conformists; he was expected to preach in a church near CAMBRIDGE; and a student of that university, not remarkable for sobriety, observing a concourse of people, was induced by curiosity to hear 'the tinker prate;' but the discourse made an unexpected impression on his mind; he embraced every future opportunity of hearing Mr. BUNYAN, and at length became an eminent preacher in CAMBRIDGESHIRE.

When the restoration took place, and, contrary to equity, engagements, and sound policy, the laws were framed and executed with a severity evidently intended to exclude every man, who scrupled the least tittle of the doctrine, liturgy, discipline, or government of the established church, Mr. BUNYAN was one of the first that suffered by them: for being courageous and unreserved, he went on in his ministerial work without any disguise; and Nov. 12, 1660, he was apprehended by a warrant from Justice WINGATE at HARLINGTON, near BEDFORD, with sixty other persons, and committed to the county jail. Security was offered for his appearance at the sessions; but it was refused, as his sureties would not consent that he should be restricted from preaching. He was accordingly confined till the quarter-sessions, when his indictment stated,—'That JOHN BUNYAN, of the town of BEDFORD, laborer, had *devilishly* and *perniciously* abstained from coming to church to hear divine service; and was a common upholder of several unlawful meetings and conventicles, to the great *disturbance* and *distraction* of the good subjects of this kingdom, contrary to the laws of our sovereign lord the King.' The facts charged upon him in this absurd indictment were never proved; as no witnesses were produced. He had confessed, in conversation with the magistrates, that he was a dissenter, and had preached: these words being considered as equivalent to conviction, were recorded against him; and as he refused to conform, he was sentenced to perpetual banishment. This sentence indeed was not executed: but he was confined in BEDFORD jail more than twelve years, notwithstanding several attempts were made to obtain his deliverance.

During this tedious imprisonment, or at least part of it, he had no books, except a Bible and FOX's Martyrology: yet thus circumstanced, he penned the PILGRIM'S PROGRESS, and many other treatises! He was only thirty-two years of age, when he was imprisoned; he had spent his youth in the most disadvantageous manner imaginable, and he had been no more than five years a member of the church at BEDFORD, and less time a preacher of the gospel: yet in this admired allegory he appears to have been most intimately acquainted with all the variety of characters, which ministers, long employed in the sacred service, and eminent for judgment and sagacity, have observed among professors or opposers of evangelical truth!

No fewer than sixty Dissenters and two ministers were confined with Mr. BUNYAN in this jail! and as some were discharged, others were committed during the time of his imprisonment! But this painful situation afforded him an opportunity of privately exercising his ministry to good effect. He learned in prison to make tagged thread laces in the intervals of his other labors; and by this employment he provided in the most unexceptionable manner for himself and his family. He seems to have been endued with extraordinary patience and courage, and to have experienced abundant consolations, while enduring these hardships: he was, however, sometimes distressed about his family, especially his eldest daughter, who was blind; but in these trying seasons he received comfort from meditating on the promises of God's word.[1]

He was at some times favored by the jailors, and permitted to see his family and friends; and, during the former part of his imprisonment, he was even allowed to go out occasionally, and once to take a journey to LONDON, probably to see whether any legal redress might be obtained; according to some intimations given by Sir MATTHEW HALE, when petitions in his favor were laid before the judges. But this indulgence of the jailor exposing him to great danger, Mr. BUNYAN was afterwards more closely confined. Hence I suppose has arisen the opinion, which commonly prevails, that he was imprisoned at *different times:* but he seems never to have been set at liberty, and then recommitted; though his hardships and restraints were greater at one time than at another.

In the last year of his imprisonment, (A.D. 1671) he was chosen pastor of the dissenting church at BEDFORD; though it does not appear what opportunity he could have of exercising

1 Jeremiah 15:11, 49:11.

his pastorale office, except within the precincts of the jail. He was however liberated soon after, through the good offices of Dr. BARLOW, bishop of LINCOLN, after many fruitless attempts had been made for that purpose. Thus terminated his tedious, severe, and even illegal imprisonment, which had given him abundant opportunity for the exercise of patience and meekness; and which seems to have been over-ruled both for his own spiritual improvement, and the furtherance of the gospel; by leading him to study, and to form habits of close reflection, and accurate investigation of various subjects, in order to pen his several treatises: when probably he would neither have thought so deeply, nor written so well, had he been more at ease and at liberty.

A short time after his enlargement, he built a meeting house at BEDFORD, by the voluntary contributions of his friends; and here he statedly preached to large auditories, till his death, without meeting with any remarkable molestation. He used to come up to LONDON every year, where he preached among the non-conformists with great acceptance; and it is said that Dr. OWEN frequently attended on these occasions, and expressed his approbation in very decided language. He likewise made stated circuits into other parts of ENGLAND; and animated his brethren to bear the cross patiently, to obey God rather then man, and to leave all consequences with him. He was at the same time peculiarly attentive to the temporal wants of those who suffered for conscience sake, and of the sick or afflicted: and he employed his influence very successfully, in reconciling differences among professors of the gospel, and thus preventing disgraceful and burdensome litigations. He was very exact in family religion, and the instruction of his children; being principally concerned for their spiritual interests, and comparatively indifferent about their temporal prosperity. He therefore declined the liberal proposal of a wealthy citizen of LONDON, to take his son as an apprentice without any premium, saying, 'God did not send me to advance my family, but to preach the gospel;'—probably disliking the business or situation as unfavorable to piety.

Nothing material is recorded concerning him, between his enlargement in 1672, and his death in 1688. It is said, that he clearly saw through the designs of the court in favor of popery, when the indulgence was granted to the Dissenters, by

James II, in 1687: but that he advised his brethren to avail themselves of the sunshine, by diligent endeavors to spread the gospel, and to prepare for an approaching storm by fasting and prayer. The next year he took a journey in very bad weather from LONDON to READING, BERKS, to make up a breach between a father and son, with whom he had some acquaintance; and having happily effected his last work and labor of love, he returned to his lodgings on SNOW-HILL, apparently in good health, but very wet with the heavy rain that was then falling: and soon after he was seized with a fever, which in ten days terminated his useful life. He bore his malady with great patience and composure, and died in a very comfortable and triumphant manner, Aug. 31, 1688, aged sixty years; after having exercised his ministry about thirty-two. He lies buried in BUNHILL FIELDS, where a tombstone to his memory may still be seen. He was twice married: by his first wife, he had four children, one of which, a daughter named MARY, who was blind, died before him. He was married to his second wife A.D. 1658, two years before his imprisonment, by whom he seems not to have had any children. She survived him about four years. Concerning the other branches of his family we have not been able to gain any information.

Mr. BUNYAN was tall and broad set, though not corpulent: he had a ruddy complexion, with sparkling eyes, and hair inclining to red, but in his old age sprinkled with grey. His whole appearance was plain, and his dress always simple and unaffected. He published sixty tracts, which equalled the number of years he lived. The PILGRIM'S PROGRESS had passed through more than fifty editions in 1784.

His character seems to have been uniformly good, from the time when he was brought acquainted with the blessed gospel of CHRIST: and though his countenance was rather stern and his manner rough; yet he was very mild, modest, and affable, in his behavior. He was backward to speak much, except on particular occasions, and remarkably averse to boasting; ready to submit to the judgment of others, and disposed to forgive injuries, to follow peace with all men, and to employ himself as a peace-maker: yet he was steady to his principles, and bold in reproving sin without respect of persons. Many slanders were spread concerning him during the course of his ministry, some of which he refuted: they have, however all died away; and no one now pretends to say any thing to his disadvantage, except as a firm attachment to his creed and practice, as a Calvinist, a Dissenter, and an Antipoedo-baptist, has been called bigotry; and as the account given of his own experience has been mis-understood or misrepresented.

He was undoubtedly endued with extraordinary natural talents; his understanding, discernment, memory, invention, and imagination, were remarkably sound and vigorous: so that he made very great proficiency in the knowledge of scriptural divinity, though brought up in ignorance; but he never made such progress in human learning.—Even such persons, as did not favor his religious principles, have done ample justice to his mental powers. The celebrated Dr. JOHNSON ranks the PILGRIM'S PROGRESS among a very few books indeed, of which the reader, when he comes to the conclusion, wishes they had been longer; and allows it to rank high among the works of original genius.[1] But it is above all things wonderful, that BUNYAN's imagina-tion, fertile and vigorous in a very great degree, and wholly untutored by the rules of learning, should in this instance have been so disciplined by sound judgement, and deep acquain-tance with the Scripture, as to produce, in the form of an alle-gory, one of the fairest and most unexceptionable treatises of the system of Calvinism, that can be found in the ENGLISH language! In several of his other publications his imagination frequently carried him beyond just bounds: but here he avoids all extremes, and seems not to deviate either to the right hand or to the left. Perhaps, as he was himself liable to depression of spirit, and had passed through deep distresses, the view he gives of the Pilgrim's temptations may be too gloomy: but he has shown in the course of the work, that this arose principally from inadequate views of evangelical truth, and the want of Christian communion, with the benefits to be derived from the counsels of a faithful minister.

---

1 PIOZZI's Anecdotes of JOHNSON.—BOSWELL's Life of JOHNSON, vol. ii. p. 97. 2d. edit.

CHAPTER I

THE DEN AND THE DREAMER

As I walked through the wilderness of this world, I lighted on a certain place where was a den.—Mr. Bunyan was confined, at different times, about twelve years in Bedford jail, for exercising his ministry contrary to the statutes then in force. This was 'the den, in which he slept and dreamed:' here he penned this instructive allegory, and many other useful works, which evince that he was neither soured nor disheartened by persecution. The Christian, who understands what usage he ought to expect in this evil world, comparing our present measure of religious liberty with the rigors of that age, will see abundant cause for gratitude; but they, who are disposed to complain, can never be at a loss for topics, while so much is amiss among all ranks and orders of men, and in the conduct of every individual.

I dreamed, and, behold, I saw a man clothed with rags standing in a certain place.—The allegory opens with a description of the principal character to which it relates. The view, which the author in his dream had of him, as 'clothed in rags,' implies that all men are sinners, in their dispositions, affections and conduct; that their supposed virtues are radically defective, and worthless in the sight of God; that the pilgrim has discovered this in his own case, so that he perceives his own righteousness to be insufficient for justification, even as sordid rags would be unsuitable raiment for those who stand before kings. His 'face turned from his own house' represents the sinner convinced that it is absolutely necessary to subordinate all other concerns to the care of his immortal soul, and to renounce every thing which interferes with that grand object: this makes him lose his former relish for the pleasures of sin, and even for the most lawful temporal satisfactions, while he trembles at the thought of impending destruction. (Hebrews 11:8, 24–27.) 'The book in his hand,' etc. instructs us, that sinners discover their real state and character, by reading and believing the Scriptures; that their first attention is often directed to the denunciations of the wrath to come contained in them, and that such persons cannot but continue to search the word of God, though their grief and alarm be increased by every perusal. The 'burden upon his back' represents that distressing sense of guilt, and fear of wrath, which deeply convinced sinners cannot shake off; 'the remembrance of their sins is grievous to them, the burden of them is intolerable:' their consciences are oppressed with guilt, even on account of those actions in which their neighbors perceive no harm; their hearts tremble at the prospect of dangers of which others have no apprehension; and they see an absolute necessity of escaping from a situation in which others live most securely: for true faith, from the very first, 'sees things that are invisible.' In one way or other, therefore, they soon manifest the earnestness of their minds, in inquiring 'what they must do to be saved.' The circumstances of these humiliating convictions exceedingly vary; but the life of faith and grace always begins with them: and they, who are wholly strangers to this experience, are Christians only in name and form:—

> 'He knows no hope, who never knew a fear.'
> *Cowper.*

In this plight, therefore, he went home, and restrained himself as long as he could, that his wife and children should not perceive his distress.—The contempt or indignation, which worldly people express towards those who are distressed in conscience, commonly induces them to conceal their inquietude as long as they can, even from their relatives; but this soon becomes impracticable. Natural affection also, connected with a view of the extreme danger to which a man sees the objects of his most tender attachments exposed, but of which they have no apprehensions, will extort such earnest representations, warnings, and entreaties, as are here expressed. The city of Destruction (as it is afterwards called) signifies this present evil world, as doomed to the flames; or the condition of careless sinners, immersed in secular pursuits and pleasures, neglecting eternal things, and exposed to the unquenchable fire of hell, 'at the day of judgment and perdition of ungodly men.' They who are ignorant of the Scriptures, and unaccustomed to compare their own conduct with the Divine law, will be amazed at such discourse; and, instead of duly regarding the warnings given them, will commonly ascribe them to enthusiasm or insanity; and as prophets, apostles, and the Son of God himself, were looked upon in this light by their contemporaries, we may be sure that no prudence, excellence, or benevolence, can exempt the consistent believer from the trial. Near relations will generally be the first to form this opinion of his case; and will devise various expedients to quiet his mind: diversions, company, feastings, absence from serious friends or books, will be prescribed: and by these means a false peace often succeeds a transient alarm. But when a genuine humiliating discovery of the evil and desert of sin has been made to the soul, such expedients will not alleviate, but increase, the anguish; and will be followed by still greater earnestness about a man's own salvation, and that of others. This commonly strengthens prejudice, and induces obduracy: and contemptuous pity gives place to resentment, ill usage, derision, or neglect. The disconsolate believer will then be driven into retirement, and relieve his burdened mind by reading the Scriptures, and meditating on his doleful case, with compassionate prayers for his despisers: and thus he sows in tears that seed from which the harvest of his future joy will surely be produced.

Now I saw, upon a time, when he was walking in the fields, that he was (as he was wont) reading in his book, and greatly distressed in his mind.—The Scriptures are indeed sufficient to make us wise unto salvation, as well as to show us our guilt and danger; yet the Lord commonly uses the ministry of his servants to direct, into the way of peace, even those who have previously discovered their lost condition. Though convinced of the necessity of escaping from impending ruin, they hesitate, not knowing what to do, till Providence brings them acquainted with some faithful preacher of the Gospel, whose instructions afford an explicit answer to their secret inquiries after the way of salvation.

Then said Evangelist, If this be thy condition, why

standest thou still?—The able minister of Christ will deem it necessary to enforce the warning, 'flee from the wrath to come,' even upon those who are alarmed about their souls; because this is the proper way of exciting them to diligence and decision, and of preserving them from procrastination. They, therefore, who would persuade such persons, that their fears are groundless, their guilt far less than they suppose, and their danger imaginary, use the most effectual means of soothing them into a fatal security. Nor can any discoveries of heinous guilt or helpless ruin in themselves produce despondency, provided the salvation of the Gospel be fully exhibited, and proposed to them.

The man therefore read it, and looking upon Evangelist very carefully, said, Wither must I flee?—The awakened sinner may be incapable for a time of perceiving the way of salvation by faith in Christ; for divine illumination is often very gradual. Thus, though the pilgrim could not see the gate, when Evangelist pointed it out to him, he thought he could discern the shining light. Upright inquirers attend to the general instructions and encouragements of Scripture, and the declarations of the pardoning mercy of God; which by degrees lead them to the knowledge of Christ, and to faith in him: for, as our author says in a marginal note, 'Christ, and the way to him, cannot be found without the word.' Thus instructed, the pilgrim 'began to run;' for no persuasions or considerations can induce the man, who is duly in earnest about salvation, to neglect those things which he knows to be his present duty: but it must be expected that carnal relations will oppose this, especially as it appears to them destructive of all their prospects of worldly advantage. The following lines are here subjoined to a very rude engraving:—

> 'Christian no sooner leaves the world, but meets
> Evangelist, who lovingly him greets
> With tidings of another; and doth show
> Him how to mount to that from this below.'

The neighbors also came out to see him run.—The attention of numbers is in general excited when one of their companions in sin and vanity engages in religion and forsakes the party. He soon becomes the topic of conversation among them: their minds are variously affected; some ridicule, others rail, threaten, attempt force, or employ artifice, to withdraw him from his purpose; according to their different dispositions, situations, or relations to him. Most of them, however, soon desist, and leave him to his choice. But two characters are not so easily shaken off; these our author has named Obstinate and Pliable, to denote their opposite propensities. The former, through a resolute pride and stoutness of heart, persists in attempting to bring back the new convert to his worldly pursuits; the latter, from a natural easiness of temper and susceptibility of impression, is pliant to persuasion, and readily consents to make a profession of religion.

The subsequent dialogue admirably illustrates the characters of the speakers. Christian (for so he is henceforth called) is firm, decided, bold, and sanguine:—Obstinate is profane, scornful, self-sufficient, and disposed to contemn God's word, when it interferes with his worldly interests:—Pliable is yielding, and easily induced to engage in things, of which he understands neither the nature nor the consequences. Christian's plain warnings and earnest entreaties; Obstinate's contempt of believers, as 'crazy-headed coxcombs,' and his exclamation when Pliable inclines to be a pilgrim, 'What, more fools still?' are admirably characteristic; and show that such things are peculiar to no age or place, but always accompany serious godliness, as the shadow does the substance.

CHAPTER II

THE SLOUGH OF DESPOND

Now I saw in my dream, that when Obstinate was gone back, Christian and Pliable went talking over the plain.—This conversation between Christian and Pliable marks the difference in their characters, as well as the measure of the new convert's attainments. The want of a due apprehension of eternal things is evidently the primary defect of all who oppose or neglect religion; but more maturity of judgment and experience is requisite to discover, that many professors are equally strangers to a realizing view 'of the powers and terrors of what is yet unseen.' The men represented by Pliable disregard these subjects; they inquire eagerly about the good things to be enjoyed, but not in any due proportion about the way of salvation, the difficulties to be encountered, or the danger of coming short: and new converts, being zealous, sanguine, and unsuspecting, are naturally led to enlarge on the descriptions of heavenly felicity given in Scripture. As these are generally figurative or negative, such unhumbled professors, annexing carnal ideas to them, are greatly delighted; and, not being retarded by any distressing remorse and terror, or feeling the opposition of corrupt nature, they are often more zealous, and seem to proceed faster in external duties, than true converts. They take it for granted that all the privileges of the Gospel belong to them; and, being very confident, zealous, and joyful, they often censure those who are really fighting the good fight of faith. There are also systems diligently propagated, which marvelously encourage this delusion, excite a high flow of false affections, especially of a mere selfish gratitude to a supposed benefactor for imaginary benefits, which is considered as a very high attainment: till the event proves them to be like the Israelites at the Red Sea, who 'believed the Lord's words, and sang his praise; but soon forgat his works, and waited not for his counsel.' (Psalm 106:12–24.)

Just as they had ended this talk, they drew nigh to a very miry slough.—The slough of Despond represents those discouraging fears which often harass new converts. It is distinguished from the alarms which induced Christian to leave the city, and 'flee from the wrath to come:' for the anxious apprehensions of one who is diligently seeking salvation are very different from those which excited him to inquire after it. The latter are reasonable and useful, and arise from faith in God's word: but the former are groundless; they result from remaining ignorance, inattention and unbelief, and greatly retard the pilgrim in his progress. They should also be carefully distinguished from those doubts and discouragements, which assault the established Christian; for these are generally the consequence of negligence, or yielding to temptation; whereas new converts fall into their despondings, when most diligent, according to the light they have received: and if some conscientious persons seem to meet with this slough in every part of their pilgrimage, it arises from an immature judgment, erroneous sentiments, or peculiar temptations. When the diligent student of the Scriptures obtains such an acquaintance with the perfect holiness of God, the spirituality of his law, the inexpressible evil of sin, and his own obligations and transgressions, as greatly exceeds the measure in which he discerns the free and full salvation of the Gospel, his humiliation will verge nearer and nearer to despondency. This, however, is not essential to repentance, but arises from misapprehension; though few in proportion wholly escape it. The *mire* of the slough represents that idea which desponding persons entertain of themselves and their situation, as altogether vile and loathsome; and their confessions and self-abasing complaints, which render them contemptible in the opinion of others. As every attempt to rescue themselves discovers to them more of the latent evil of their hearts, they seem to grow worse and worse; and, for want of a clear understanding of the Gospel, they have no firm ground to tread on, and know neither where they are, or what they must do. But how could Pliable fall into this slough, seeing he had no such views of God or his law, of himself, or of sin, as this condition seems to presuppose? To this it may be answered, that men can hardly associate with religious persons, and hear their discourse, confessions, and complaints, or become acquainted with any part of Scripture, without making some alarming and mortifying discoveries concerning themselves. These transient convictions taking place when they fancied they were about to become very good, and succeeding to great self-complacency, constitute a grievous disappointment; and they ascribe their uneasiness to the new doctrine they have heard. But, though Pliable fell into the slough, Christian 'by reason of his burden' sank the deepest; for the true believer's humiliation for sin tends greatly to increase his fear of wrath. Superficial professors, expecting the promised happiness without trouble or suffering, are often very angry at those who were the means of inducing them to think of religion; as if they had deceived them: and, being destitute of true faith, their only object is, at any rate to get rid of their uneasiness. This is a species of stony-ground hearers abounding in every part of the church, who are offended and fall away, by means of a little *inward* disquietude, before any *outward* tribulation arises because of the word.

Still he endeavored to struggle to that side of the slough that was farthest from his own house, and next to the Wicket-gate.—Christian dreaded the doom of his city more than the slough. Many persons, under deep distress of conscience, are afraid of relief, lest it should prove delusive. Deliverance from wrath and the blessings of salvation appear to them so valuable, that all else is comparatively trivial. Desponding fears may connect with their religious diligence; but despair would be the consequence of a return to their former course of sin. If they perish, therefore, it shall be whilst earnestly struggling, under deep discouragement, after that salvation for which their souls even faint within them. Their own efforts, indeed, fail to extricate them: but in due time the Lord will send them assistance. This is described by the allegorical person named Help, who may represent the instruments by which they receive encouragement: a service in which it is a privilege to be employed! Fear is also personified: in the midst of the new convert's discourse on the joys of heaven, fears of wrath often cast him into despondency, while he so thinks of the terrors of the Lord, as to overlook his precious promises.

And he said unto me, This miry slough is such a place as cannot be mended: it is the descent whither the scum and filth that attends conviction for sin doth continually run.—This account of the slough, which our author in his vision received from Help, coincides with the preceding explanation. Increasing knowledge produces deeper self-abasement: hence discouraging fears arise in men's minds, lest they should at last perish; and objections against themselves continually accumulate till they fall into habitual despondency, unless they constantly attend to the encouragements of the Scripture, or, in the apostle's language, have their 'feet shod with the preparation of the Gospel of peace.' As this state of mind is distressing and enfeebling in itself, and often furnishes enemies with a plausible objection to religion, the servants of God have always attempted to preserve humble inquirers from it, by various scriptural instructions and consolatory topics: yet their success is not adequate to their wishes; for the Lord is pleased to permit numbers to be thus discouraged, in order to detect false professors, and to render the upright more watchful and humble. Our author in a marginal note, explains the steps to mean, 'the promises of forgiveness and acceptance to life by faith in Christ;' which includes the general invitations, and the various encouragements given in Scripture to all who seek the salvation of the Lord, and diligently use the appointed means. It was evidently his opinion, that the path from destruction to life lies by this slough; and that none are indeed in the narrow way, who had neither struggled through it, nor gone over it by means of the steps. The 'change of weather' seems to denote those seasons when peculiar temptations, exciting sinful passions, perplex the minds of new converts; and so, losing sight of the promises, they sink into despondency during humiliating experiences: but faith in Christ, and in the mercy of God through him, sets the pilgrim's feet on good ground.

So his neighbors came to visit him; and some of them called him wise man for coming back.—They, who affect to despise real Christians, often both express and feel great contempt for those that cast off their profession; such men are unable, for a time, to resume their wonted confidence among their former companions; and this excites them to pay court to them by reviling and deriding those whom they have forsaken.

CHAPTER III

WORLDLY WISEMAN

The gentleman's name that met him was Mr. Worldly Wiseman.—The wise men of this world carefully notice those who begin to turn their thoughts to religion, and attempt to counteract their convictions before the case becomes desperate: from their desponding fears they take occasion to insinuate that they are deluded or disordered in their minds; that they make too much ado about religion; and that a decent regard to it (which is all that is requisite) consists with the enjoyment of this life, and even conduces to secular advantage. Worldly Wiseman, therefore, is a person of consequence, whose superiority gives him influence over poor pilgrims: he is a reputable and successful man; prudent, sagacious, and acquainted with mankind; moral and religious in his way, and qualified to give the very best counsel to those who wish to serve both God and Mammon: but he is decided in his judgment against all kinds and degrees of religion, which interfere with a man's worldly interest, disquiet his mind, or spoil his relish for outward enjoyments. He resides at Carnal Policy, a great town near the city of Destruction: for worldly prudence, modelling a man's religion, is as ruinous as open vice and impiety; though it be very prevalent among decent and virtuous people. Such men attend to the reports that are circulated about the conversion of their neighbors, and often watch their opportunity of entering into discourse with them.

Worldly Wiseman: How now, good fellow, whither away after this burdened manner?—There is great beauty in this dialogue, arising from the exact regard to character preserved throughout. Indeed this forms one of our author's peculiar excellencies; as it is a very difficult attainment, and always manifests a superiority of genius. The self-satisfaction of Worldly Wiseman, his contempt of Christian's capacity, sentiments, and pursuits; his affected sneering compassion, and his censure of Evangelist's advice; his representation of the dangers and hardships of the way, and of 'the desperate ventures of religious people to obtain they know not what:' and his confident assumption that Christian's concern arose from weakness of intellect, 'meddling with things too high' for him, hearkening to bad counsel (that is reading the word of God, and attending to the preaching of the Gospel), and from distraction, as the natural consequence, are most admirably characteristic. His arguments also are very specious, though wholly deduced from worldly considerations. He does not say, that Evangelist had not pointed out the way of salvation, or that wicked men are not in danger of future misery; but he urges, that so much concern about sin and the eternal world takes men off from a proper regard to their secular interests, to the injury of their families; that it prevents their enjoying comfort in domestic life, or in other providential blessings; that it leads them into perilous and distressing situations, of which their first terrors and despondings are only an earnest; that a troubled conscience may be quieted in a more expeditious and easy manner; and that they may obtain credit, comfort, and manifold advantages, by following prudent counsel. On the other hand, Christian not only speaks according to his name, but consistently with the character of a young convert. He makes no secret of his disquietude and terrors, and declares, without reserve, the method in which he sought relief. He owns, that he had lost his relish for every earthly comfort, and he desires to receive good counsel: but while he is prepared to withstand all persuasions to return home, he is not upon his guard against the insidious proposal of his carnal counsellor. He fears the wrath to come more than all the dreadful things which had been mentioned: but his earnestness to get present relief exposes him to the danger of seeking it in an unwarranted way. He has obtained from the Scriptures a conviction of his guilt and danger; but, not having also learned the instructions of life, he does not discern the fatal tendency of the plausible advice given him by so reputable a person. Every one, who has been in the way of making observations on these matters, must perceive how exactly this suits the case of numbers, when first brought to mind the one thing needful.

Worldly Wiseman: Why, in yonder village (the village is named Morality) there dwells a gentleman whose name is Legality.—The village Morality, is the emblem of that large company, who in nations favored with revelation abstain from scandalous vices, and practise reputable duties, without any true fear or love of God, or regard to his authority or glory. This, connected with a system of notions, and a stint of external worship, is substituted in the place of Christianity: but it is faulty in its principle, measure, and object; it results wholly from self-love; is restricted to the outward observance of some precepts selected from the Scriptures; and aims principally at the acquisition of reputation, distinction, or temporal advantages, with no more than a subordinate respect even to the interests of eternity: it is destitute of humility, delight, impartiality, and universality in obedience; it leaves the heart in the possession of some worldly idol, and never advances a man to the rank of a spiritual worshipper, or renders him meet for the peculiar pleasures of heaven. Yet this mutilated kind of religion draws multitudes off from attending either to the holy requirements of the law, or to the humbling doctrines of the Gospel. The most noted inhabitant of this village does not derive his name, Legality, from making the law of God the rule of his conduct (for 'by the law is the knowledge of sin,' which tends to increase the convinced sinner's distress), but from his teaching men to depend on a defective obedience to a small part of the law, explained and lowered, according to the method of the scribes and pharisees. Such teachers, however, are admired by the wise men of this world, and are deemed very skilful in relieving troubled consciences, and recovering men from religious distractions. His son Civility is the emblem of those, who persuade themselves and others, that a decent, benevolent, and obliging behavior, will secure men from all future punishment, and insure an inheritance in heaven, if indeed there be any such place! Such counsellors can ease the consciences of ignorant persons, when superficially alarmed, almost as well as those who superadd a form of godliness, a few doctrinal opinions, and a regard to some precepts of the Gospel. Both are nigh at hand in every place; and the wise men of this world are ever ready to direct convinced sinners to seek relief from them: they allow, that it is better for those who have been immoral and profligate to reform their lives; for this will meet with the approbation of their relatives, and conduce to their advantage, while the strait gate and narrow way would prove their ruin. Most pilgrims are assailed by such counsellors: and many are not able to detect the fallacy of their reasonings till their own folly corrects them.

Worldly Wiseman: Do you see yonder high hill?— Christian must go past mount Sinai to the village Morality; not that such men, as depend on their own reformation and good works, pay a due regard to the holy law which was delivered from that mountain (for 'they are alive without the law'); but because they substitute their own scanty obedience in the place of Christ's righteousness and atonement. They, who are not duly humbled and enlightened, perceiving little danger, pass on quietly and securely: but the sinner, who is deeply convinced of his guilt, finds every attempt 'to establish his own righteousness' entirely abortive: the more narrowly he compares his conduct and character with the holy law, the greater is his alarm: and he trembles lest its curses should immediately fall upon him, with vengeance more tremendous than the most awful thunder. Then the counsels of worldly wisdom appear in their true light, and the sinner is prepared to welcome the Gospel of free salvation: but if the minister, whose instructions he had forsaken, meet him, his terror will unite with conscious shame; and he will even be tempted to shun his faithful friend, through fear of his merited reproofs.

Then said Evangelist, Stand still a little, that I may show thee the words of God.—Our author judged it right, in dealing with persons under great terror of conscience, to aim rather at preparing them for solid peace, than hastily to give them comfort. Men may be greatly dismayed, and in some degree truly humbled, yet not be duly sensible of the aggravation and degree of their guilt. In this case, further instructions, as to the nature and heinousness of their offences, are needful to excite them to proper diligence and self-denial, and to prepare them for solid peace and comfort. Whereas, a well-meant, compassionate, but injudicious, method, of proposing consolatory topics indiscriminately to all under trouble of conscience, lulls many into a fatal sleep; and gives others a transient peace, which soon terminates in deep despondency: like a wound, hastily skinned over by an ignorant practitioner, instead of being soundly cured by the patient attention of a skilful surgeon. The communication of more knowledge may, indeed, augment a man's terror and distress; but it will produce deeper humiliation, and thus effectually warn him against carnal counsellors and legal dependences. Whatever may be generally thought of 'turning aside' from the Gospel, it is a direct refusal to hearken to Christ; and they who do so, run into misery, and leave the way of peace, to the hazard of their souls; even though moral decency and formal piety be the result. (Galatians 5:4.) Such denunciations are despised by the stout-hearted, but the contrite in spirit, when conscious of this guilt, are cast by them into the deepest distress; so that they would fall into despair did not the ministers of Christ encourage them by evangelical topics. The following lines are here inserted, as before, in the old editions:—

'When Christians unto carnal men give ear,
Out of their way they go, and pay for't dear:
For Master Worldly Wiseman can but show
A saint the way to bondage and to woe.'

He so called; partly because he savoreth only of the doctrine of this world, (therefore he always goes to the town of Morality to church).—Worldly Wiseman goes to church at the town of Morality: for such men support their confidence and reputation for religion by attending on those preachers, who substitute a proud scanty morality in place of the Gospel. This coincides with their secular views, dispositions, and interests; they avoid the cross, verily thinking they had found out the secret of reconciling the friendship of the world with the favor of God; and then they set up for teachers of the same convenient system to their neighbors!

He to whom thou wast sent for ease, being by name Legality.—When Christ had finished his work on earth, the Sinai covenant with Israel was abrogated. The Jews, therefore, by cleaving to the Mosaic law as a complex covenant of works, were left in bondage and under condemnation; and all professed Christians, who thus depend on notions, sacraments, religious duties, and morality, to the neglect of Christ and the new covenant in his blood, are entangled in the same fatal error. Legality can only lead a man to a false peace: it can never deliver a sinner from guilt, or quiet the conscience of one who is really humbled and enlightened. The Scriptures adduced by Evangelist are so pertinent and conclusive against the fashionable religion, which has at present almost super-seded the Gospel, that they can never be fairly answered: nay, the more any man considers them as the testimony of God, the greater must be his alarm (even as if he heard the voice from mount Sinai out of the midst of the fire); unless he be conscious of having renounced every other confidence, to 'flee for refuge to lay hold on the hope set before us' in the Gospel. Such alarms prepare men to attend to the counsel of those who preach sal-vation by faith in Christ alone, provided there may yet be hope; of which there is no reason to doubt.

Then said Evangelist to him, Thy sin is very great, for by it thou hast committed two evils.—In attempting to encourage those who despond, we should by no means per-suade them that their sins are few or trivial, or even that they judge too hardly of their own conduct; nay, we should endeavor to convince them that their guilt is even far greater than they suppose; though not too great to be pardoned by the infinite mercy of God in Christ Jesus: for this tends to take them off more speedily from every vain attempt to justify themselves, and renders them more unreserved in relying on Christ for acceptance. In the midst of the most affectionate encourage-ments, the faithful minister must also solemnly warn young converts not to turn aside; nor can the humble ever find confi-dence or comfort, till they are conscious of having regained the way they had forsaken.

CHAPTER IV

THE WICKET-GATE

So in process of time Christian got up to the gate.—The
gate, at which Christian desired admission, represents Christ
himself, as received by the penitent sinner in all his offices, and
for all the purposes of salvation, according to the measure of
his explicit knowledge; by which he actually enters into a state
of acceptance with God. The Scriptures referred to were spoken
by our Lord himself, previous to the full revelation of his character and redemption; and may be very properly explained of a
man's finally and decidedly renouncing his worldly and sinful
pursuits, and engaging with diligence and self-denial in a life
of devotedness to God. 'The broad road leads to destruction;'
the gate by which men enter into it is wide; for we are all 'born
in sin and the children of wrath,' and 'turn every one to his own
way' of folly and transgression: but the strait gate opens into
'the narrow way that leadeth unto life;' and at this the penitent
finds admission with difficulty and conflict. As it is strait, (or,
in the language of the allegory, a wicket, or a little gate,) the
convert cannot carry along with him any of his sinful practices,
ungodly companions, worldly idols, or carnal confidences, when
he strives to enter in at it; nor can he effectually contend with
those enemies that obstruct his passage, unless he wrestle continually with God in prayer, for his gracious assistance. But,
while we advert to these things, we must not forget, that the
sinner returns to God by faith in Christ: genuine repentance
comes from him and leads to him; and the true believer not
only trusts in the Lord for salvation, but also seeks his liberty
and happiness in his service. To enter in this manner, by Christ

the door, is so contrary to man's pride and lusts, to the course of the world, and to the temptations of the devil, that *striving* or *wrestling* is more necessary in this than it can be conceived to be in any other kind of conversion. Various things commonly precede this unreserved acceptance of Christ, in the experience of those who are born of God; but they are not easily distinguishable from many temporary convictions, impressions, and starts of devotion, which evidently vanish and come to nothing. Yet even this is judiciously distinguished by our author from that view of the cross by which Christian was delivered from his burden, for reasons which will speedily be stated. The following lines are here inserted, under an engraving:—

'He that would enter in, must first without
Stand knocking at the gate, nor need he doubt
That is a knocker, but to enter in:
For God can love him, and forgive his sin.'

At last there came a grave person to the gate, named Good-will.—Good-will seems to be an allegorical person, the emblem of the compassionate love of God to sinners, in and through Jesus Christ (Luke 2:14). He 'came from heaven to do the will of him that sent him,' and 'he will in no wise cast out any that come to him,' either on account of their former sins, or their present mistakes, infirmities, evil propensities and habits, or peculiar temptations. 'He waits to be gracious,' till sinners apply by earnest persevering prayer for his salvation; and even the preparation of heart which leads to this is not requisite to induce the Lord to receive them, but to make them willing to apply to him. Numbers give themselves no concern about their souls; others, after convictions, turn back with Pliable, or finally cleave to the counsels of worldly wisdom: but all, who come to Christ with a real desire of his whole salvation, are cordially welcomed: over them angels rejoice, and in them the Redeemer 'sees of the travail of his soul and is satisfied.' So that inquirers are greatly mistaken when they fear lest Christ should reject them; since they need only dread being tempted to reject him, or being partial and hypocritical in their application to him.

So when Christian was stepping in, the other gave him a pull.—As sinners become more decided in applying to Christ, and assiduous in the means of grace, Satan, if permitted, will be more vehement in his endeavors to discourage them; that, if possible, he may induce them to desist, and so to come short of the prize. Indeed, the Lord will accomplish the good work which he hath began by his special grace; but probably the powers of darkness cannot exactly distinguish between those impressions which are the effects of regeneration, and such as result from the excitement of natural passions. It is, however, certain, that they attempt to disturb those who earnestly cry for mercy, by various suggestions, to which they were wholly strangers, while satisfied with a form of godliness: and that the Christian's grand conflict, to the end of his course, consists in surmounting the hindrances and opposition that he experiences, in keeping near to the throne of grace, by fervent, importunate, and persevering prayer.

Truly, said Christian, I have said the truth of Pliable, and if I should also say all the truth of myself, it will appear there is no betterment betwixt him and myself.— Our author here puts a very emphatical word into Christian's mouth, ('there is no *betterment* betwixt him and myself,') which later editors have changed for *difference.* This is far from an improvement, though the word be more classical: for grace had made an immense *difference* between Christian and Pliable; but the former thought his conduct equally criminal, and therefore, in respect to their deservings, there was no *betterment* betwixt them. There are many alterations of a similar nature, in which the old copies have been generally followed; but it would preclude more useful matter were they constantly noted.

Look before thee; dost thou see this narrow way? that is the way thou must go.—Christian, being admitted at the strait gate, is directed in the narrow way. In the broad road every man may choose a path suited to his inclinations, shift about to avoid difficulties, or accommodate himself to circumstances; and he will be sure of company agreeable to his taste. But Christians must follow one another in the narrow way, along the same track, surmounting difficulties, facing enemies, and bearing hardships, without any room to evade them: nor is any indulgence given to different tastes, habits, or propensities. It is, therefore, a straitened, or, as some render the word, an afflicted way; being indeed an habitual course of repentance, faith, love, self-denial, patience, and mortification to sin and the world, according to the rule of the Holy Scriptures.

Christ himself is the way, by which we come to the Father and walk with him; but true faith works by love, and 'sets us in the way of his steps.' (Psalm 85:13.) This path is also straight, as opposed to the crooked ways of wicked men (Psalm 125:5;) for it consists in an uniform regard to piety, integrity, sincerity, and kindness, at a distance from all the hypocrisies, frauds, and artifices by which ungodly men wind about, to avoid detection, keep up their credit, deceive others, or impose on themselves. The question proposed by Christian implies, that believers are more afraid of missing the way, than encountering hardships in it: and Good-will's answer, that many ways *butted* down on it, or opened into it, in various directions, shows, that the careless and self-willed are extremely liable to be deceived: but it follows, that all these ways are crooked and wide; they turn aside from the direct line of living faith and holy obedience, and are more soothing, indulgent, and pleasing to corrupt nature than the path of life; which lies straight forward, and is every where contrary to the bias of the carnal mind.

Christian asked him further, if he could not help him off with his burden that was upon his back.—A general reliance on the mercy of God by faith in Christ, accompanied with consciousness of sincerity in applying for this salvation, gives some encouragement to the convinced sinner's hope; and transient joys are often vouchsafed in a large proportion to unestablished believers: but more distinct views of the glory of the gospel are necessary to abiding peace. The young convert's consolations resemble the breaking forth of the sun in a cloudy and tempestuous day; those of the experienced Christian, the sun's more constant light in settled weather, which is not long together interrupted, though it be sometimes dimmed by intervening clouds. Believers should not, therefore, rest in such transient glimpses, but press forward to more abiding peace and joy: and, as Christ does not in general bestow this blessing on the unestablished, the endeavors of ministers to do so must be vain.

CHAPTER V

THE INTERPRETER'S HOUSE

He came at the house of the Interpreter, where he knocked over and over.—We continually meet with fresh proofs of our author's exact acquaintance with the Scriptures, his sound judgment, deep experience, and extensive observation. With great propriety he places the house of the Interpreter beyond the strait gate: for the knowledge of divine things, which precedes conversion to God by faith in Christ, is very scanty, compared with the diligent believer's subsequent attainments. A few leading truths deeply impressed on the heart and producing efficacious fears, hopes, desires, and affections, characterize the state of a new-born babe: but reliance on the mercy of God through Jesus Christ prepares him to receive further instruction: and, 'having tasted that the Lord is gracious, he desires the sincere milk of the word, that he may grow thereby.' The Interpreter is an emblem of the teaching of the Holy Spirit, according to the Scripture, by means of reading, hearing, praying, and meditating accompanied by daily experience and observation. Believers depend on this continual teaching, and are not satisfied with human instruction, but look to the fountain of wisdom, that they may be delivered from prejudice, preserved from error, and enabled to profit by the ministry of the word.

Then said the Interpreter, Come in; I will show thee that which is profitable to thee.—The condescending love of the Holy Spirit, in readily granting the desires of those who apply for his teaching, notwithstanding their sins, prejudices, and slowness of heart to understand, can never sufficiently be admired. (Psalm 143:10.) He employs men as his instruments, who, by explaining the Scriptures, may be said to 'light the candle:' but he alone efficaciously opens the mind to instruction. 'The secret of the Lord is with them that fear him.' (Psalm 25:14.) The Interpreter leads them apart to communicate to them heavenly wisdom, which is hidden from the most sagacious of worldly men. The first lesson here inculcated relates to the character of the true minister: for nothing can be more important to every one who inquires the way to heaven, than to be able to distinguish faithful pastors from hirelings, blind guides, and false teachers; who are Satan's principal agents in deceiving mankind, and in preventing the stability, consistency, and fruitfulness of believers. The portrait and its key need no explanation: but all, who sustain, or mean to assume the sacred office, should seriously examine it, clause by clause, with the Scriptures from which it is deduced; inquiring impartially how far they resemble it, and praying earnestly for more exact conformity; and every one should be extremely careful not to intrust his soul to the guidance of those who are wholly unlike this emblematic representation. For surely a slothful, frivolous, dissipated, licentious, ambitious, profane, or contentious man, in the garb of a minister, cannot safely be trusted as a guide in the way to heaven. He, who never studies, or studies any thing in preference to the Bible, cannot be qualified to 'unfold dark things to sinners!' and he, who is abundantly more careful about his income, ease, or consequence, than about the souls of his flock, cannot be followed without the most evident danger and the most inexcusable folly! For who would employ an ignorant, indolent, or fraudulent lawyer, or physician, merely because he happened to live in the same parish?

When he began to sweep, the dust began so abundantly to fly about, that Christian had almost therewith been choked.—All true believers desire sanctification, of which the moral law is the standard: yet every attempt to produce conformity in heart and life to that standard, by regarding the precepts, apart from the truths and promises, of Scripture, excites and discovers the evils which before lay dormant in the heart; according to the significant emblem here adduced. Mere moral preaching, indeed, has no such effect: because in the place of the divine law, it substitutes another rule, which is so vague, that self-flattery will enable almost any man, who is not scandalously vicious, to deem himself justified according to it: so that, instead of enmity being excited in the heart, he allows the rule by which he is approved; and loves his idea of God, because it accords so well with his own character. But, when the holy law is brought with energy to the conscience, its strictness, spirituality, and severity, awaken the latent enmity of the heart: the absolute self-denial it demands, even in the most plausible claims of self-love, its express prohibition of the darling sin, with the experienced impracticability of adequate obedience, and the awful sentence it denounces against every transgressor, concur in exciting opposition to it, and even to him who gave it. Moreover, the consciousness of a hankering after things prohibited, and a conviction of the evil of such concupiscence, induce a man to conclude that he is viler than ever; and, indeed, clearer knowledge must aggravate the guilt of every sin. A little discouragement of this kind prevails with numbers to cease from all endeavors, at least for a season; supposing that at present it is impossible for them to serve God; but others, being more deeply humbled, and taken off from all self-confidence, are thus prepared to understand and welcome the free salvation of the Gospel. The law then appears disarmed of its curse, as the rule and standard of holiness; while righteousness and strength are sought by faith in Jesus Christ: the believer is encouraged by the truths and promises of the Gospel, excited by its motives, and inclined by the Holy Spirit, to desire advancing sanctification: while by the prevalence of hope and love his inward enmity is subdued, and he delights in 'cleansing himself from all filthiness of flesh and spirit, and perfecting holiness in the fear of God.'

The name of the eldest was Passion, and the name of the other Patience.—In this instructive emblem, Passion represents the prevalence of the carnal affections over reason and religion. Whatever be the object, this dominion of the passions produces fretfulness and childish perverseness, when a man cannot obtain the imagined good his heart is set upon, which wholly relates to the present life. But this impatience of delay or disappointment is succeeded by pride, insolence, contempt of others, and inordinate momentary delight, if he be indulged with the possession of his idol. Such men may scorn believers as foolish and wretched: but they soon grow dissatisfied with success, and speedily lavish away their good things.

On the other hand, Patience is the emblem of those who quietly and meekly wait for future happiness, renouncing present things for the sake of it. True riches, honors, and pleasures, are intended for them, but not here; and as well educated little children, they simply wait for them till the appointed season, in the way of patience and obedience. Reason determines, that a greater and more permanent good hereafter is preferable to a less and fleeting enjoyment at present: faith realizes, as attainable, a felicity infinitely more valuable than all which this world can possibly propose to us: so that in this respect the life of faith is the reign of reason over passion, while unbelief makes way for the triumph of passion over reason. Nor can any thing be more essential to practical religion than an abiding conviction, that it is the only true wisdom, uniformly and cheerfully to part with every temporal good, whenever it interferes with the grand concerns of eternity.

The man stood behind the wall to maintain the fire; this is to teach thee, that it is hard for the tempted to see how this work of grace is maintained in the soul.— The doctrine of the true believer's final perseverance is here stated in so guarded a manner as to preclude every abuse of it. The emblem implies, that the soul is indeed quickened by special grace, and endued with holy affections; and this heavenly flame is not almost extinguished or covered with ashes for many years, and then revived a little at the closing scene; but it 'burns brighter and hotter,' notwithstanding the opposition of depraved nature, and the unremitted efforts of Satan to quench it; for the Lord secretly feeds it with the oil of his grace. Unbelievers can persevere in nothing but impiety or hypocrisy: when a professor remarkably loses the vigor of his affections, the reality of his conversion becomes doubtful, and he can take no warranted encouragement from the doctrine in question; but when any one grows more spiritual, zealous, humble, and exemplary, in the midst of harassing temptations, while he gives the whole glory to the Lord, he may take comfort from the assurance, that 'he shall be kept by his power, through faith, unto salvation.' Yet the way, in which the tempted are preserved, often so far exceeds their expectations, that they are a wonder to themselves: every thing seems to concur in giving Satan advantage against them, and his efforts appear very successful; yet they continue from year to year, 'cleaving with purpose of heart unto the Lord,' trusting in his mercy, and desirous of living to his glory. The instruction especially inculcated by this emblem is, an entire reliance on the secret but powerful influence of divine grace, to maintain and carry on the sanctifying work that has been begun in the soul.

He saw also upon the top thereof certain persons walking, who were clothed in all gold.—Many desire the joys and glories of heaven (according to their carnal ideas of them,) but few are willing to 'fight the good fight of faith:' yet, without this fixed purpose of heart, the result of Divine grace, profession will end in apostasy:—'the man began to build, but was not able to finish.' This is emphatically taught us by the next emblem. Salvation is altogether free and without price: but we must learn to value it so highly as to venture or suffer 'the loss of all things that we may win Christ;' or we shall not be able to break through the combined opposition of the world, the flesh, and the devil. If we fear any mischief that our enemies can attempt against us, more than coming short of salvation, we shall certainly perish, notwithstanding our notions and convictions. We should, therefore, count our cost, and pray for courage and constancy, that we may give in our names as in earnest to win the prize: then, 'putting on the whole armor of God,' and relying on his grace, we must fight our way through with patience and resolution; while many, 'being harnessed and carrying bows,' shamefully 'turn back in the day of battle.'

Now, said Christian, let me go hence. Nay, stay, said the Interpreter, till I have showed thee a little more, and after that thou shalt go on thy way.—The time, spent in acquiring knowledge and sound judgment, is not lost, though it may seem to retard a man's progress, or interfere with his more active services: and the next emblem is admirably suited to teach the young convert watchfulness and caution. Christian's discourse with the man in the iron cage sufficiently explains the author's meaning; but it has been observed by several persons, that the man's opinion of his own case, does not prove that it was indeed desperate. Doubtless these fears prevail in some cases of deep despondency, when there is every reason to conclude them groundless; and we should always propose the free grace of the Gospel to those that have sinned in the most aggravated manner, when they become sensible of their guilt and danger: yet it is an awful fact, that some are thus 'shut up under despair,' beyond relief; and 'it is impossible to renew them to repentance.' No true penitent, therefore, can be in this case: and we are commanded 'in meekness to instruct those that oppose themselves, if peradventure God will give them repentance.' But, at the same time, we should leave the doom of apparent apostates to God; and improve their example, as a warning to ourselves and others, not to venture one step in so dangerous a path. This our author has judiciously attempted, and we should be careful not to counteract his obvious intention.

Then said the Interpreter to Christian, Hast thou considered all these things? Chrisitan: Yes, and they put me in hope and fear.—Our safety consists in a due proportion of hope and fear: when devoid of hope, we resemble a ship without an anchor: when unrestrained by fear, we are like the same vessel under full sail, without ballast (1 Peter 1:13–17.) Indiscriminate censures of all fear as the result of unbelief, and unguarded commendations of strong confidence, without respect to the spirit and conduct of professors, not only lead to much self-deception, but also tend to make believers unstable, unwatchful, and even uncomfortable; for the humble often cannot attain to that confidence, that is represented almost as essential to faith; and true comfort is the effect of watchfulness, diligence, and circumspection. Upon the whole, what lessons could possibly have been selected of greater importance, or more suited to establish the new convert, than these are, which our author has most ingeniously and agreeably inculcated, under the emblem of the Interpreter's curiosities? They are indeed the principal subjects which faithful ministers enforce, publicly and in private, on all who begin to profess the Gospel; and which every true disciple of Christ daily seeks to have more clearly discovered to his mind, and more deeply impressed upon his heart.

CHAPTER VI

THE CROSS AND THE CONTRAST

Up this way, therefore, did burdened Christian run, but not without great difficulty, because of the load on his back.—Divine illumination in many respects tends to quicken the believer's hopes and fears, and to increase his earnestness and diligence; but nothing can finally relieve him from his burden, except the clear discovery of the nature and glory of redemption. With more general views of the subject, and an implicit reliance on God's mercy through Jesus Christ, the humbled sinner enters the way of life, which is walled by salvation: yet he is oppressed with an habitual sense of guilt, and often bowed down with fears, till 'the Comforter, who glorifies Christ, receives of his, and shows it to him' (John 16:14.) When in this divine light the soul contemplates the Redeemer's cross, and discerns more clearly his love to lost sinners in thus dying for them; the motive and efficacy of his intense sufferings; the glory of the Divine perfections harmoniously displayed in this surprising expedient for saving the lost; the honor of the Divine law and government, and the evil and desert of sin, most energetically proclaimed in this way of pardoning transgressors and reconciling enemies; and the perfect freeness and sufficiency of this salvation; then 'his conscience is purged from dead works to serve the living God,' by a simple reliance on the atoning blood of Emmanuel. This deliverance from the burden of guilt is in some respects final, as to the well-instructed and consistent believer; his former sins are buried, no more to be his terror and distress. He will indeed be deeply humbled under a sense of his guilt, and sometimes he may question his acceptance; but his distress, before he understood the way of deliverance, was habitual, except in a few transient seasons of relief, and often oppressed him when most diligent and watchful; but now he is only burdened when he has been betrayed into sin, or when struggling with peculiar temptations; and he constantly finds relief by looking to the cross. Many indeed never attain to this habitual peace: this is the effect of remaining ignorance, error, or negligence, which scriptural instructions are the proper means of obviating. But it was not probable that our author should, so to speak, draw the character of his hero from the lowest order of hopeful professors; it may rather call for our admiration, that, in an allegory (which is the peculiar effort of a vigorous imagination) he was preserved, by uncommon strength of mind and depth of judgment, from stating Christian's experience above the general attainments of consistent believers, under solid instructions.

It was very surprising to him that the sight of the cross should thus ease him of his burden. He looked, therefore, and looked again.—Christian's tears, amidst his gladness, intimate that deliverance from guilt, by faith in the atoning sacrifice of Christ, tends to increase humiliation, sorrow for sin, and abhorrence of it; though it mingles even those affections with a sweet and solid pleasure. By the 'three shining ones,' the author might allude to the ministration of angels as conducive to the comfort of the heirs of salvation; but he could not mean to ascribe Christian's confidence to any impressions, or suggestions of texts to him by a voice, or in a dream; any more than he intended, by his views of the cross, to sanction the account that persons of heated imagination have given, of their having seen one hang on a cross, covered with blood, who told them their sins were pardoned; while it has been evident, that they never understood the spiritual glory, or the sanctifying tendency of the doctrine of a crucified Savior. Such things are the mere delusions of enthusiasm, from which our author was remarkably free: but the nature of an allegory led him to this method of describing the happy change that takes place in the pilgrim's experience, when he obtains peace and joy in believing. His uniform doctrine sufficiently shows that he considers spiritual apprehensions of the nature of the atonement as the only source of genuine peace and comfort. And, as the 'mark in the forehead' plainly signifies the renewal of the soul to holiness, so that the mind of Christ may appear in the outward conduct, connected with an open profession of faith, while the 'roll with a seal upon it' denotes such an assurance of acceptance, as appears most clear and satisfactory, when the believer most attentively compares his views, experiences, desires, and purposes, with the Holy Scriptures; so he could not possibly intend to ascribe such effects to any other agent than the Holy Spirit; who by enabling a man to exercise all filial affections towards God in an enlarged degree, as 'the Spirit of adoption bears witness' with his conscience, that God is reconciled to him, having pardoned all his sins; that he is justified by faith in the righteousness of Emmanuel; and that he is a child of God, and an heir of heaven. These things are clear and intelligible to those who have experienced this happy change; and the abiding effects of their joy in the Lord, upon their dispositions and conduct (like the impression of the seal after the wax is cooled) distinguish it from the confidence and comfort of hypocrites and enthusiasts. It must, however, continue to be 'the secret of the Lord, with them that fear him,' 'hidden manna,' and 'a white stone, having in it a new name written, which no man knoweth saving he that receiveth it.' Psalm 25:14; Revelation 2:17. Here again we meet with an engraving, and the following lines:—

> 'Who's this? The Pilgrim. How? 'Tis very true
> Old things are past away! all's become new.
> Strange! he's another man, upon my word;
> They be fine feathers that make a fine bird.'

I saw then in my dream, that he went on thus, even until he came at a bottom, where he saw, a little out of the way, three men fast asleep, with fetters upon their heels.—We were before informed, that other ways 'butted down upon' the straight way; and the connection of the allegory required the introduction of various characters, besides that of the true believer. Many may outwardly walk in the ways of religion, and seem to be pilgrims, who are destitute of those 'things which accompany salvation.' The three allegorical persons next introduced are nearly related; they appear to be pilgrims, but are a little out of the way, asleep, and fettered. Many of this description are found, where the truth is preached, as well as elsewhere: they hear and learn to talk about the Gospel; have transient convictions, which are soon quieted; cleave to the world, and rest more securely in the bondage of sin and Satan, by means of their profession of religion. They reject or pervert all instruction, hate all trouble, yet are confident that every thing is and will be well with them, while teachers, after their own hearts, lull them with a siren's song, by confounding the form with the power of godliness; and if any one attempt, in the most affectionate manner to warn them of their danger, they answer (according to the tenor of the words here used,) 'Mind your own business; we see no danger; you shall not disturb our composure, or induce us to make so much ado about religion: see to yourselves, and leave us to ourselves.' Thus they sleep on till death and judgment awake them.

Yet he was troubled to think, that men in that danger should so little esteem the kindness of him that so freely offered to help them.—The true Christian will always be troubled when he thinks of the vain confidence of many professors: but he is more surprised by it at first than afterwards; for he sets out with the idea, that all apparently religious people sincerely seek the salvation of God: but at length experience draws his attention to those parts of Scripture which mention tares among the wheat, and foolish virgins among the wise. Formalist and Hypocrisy soon come in his way; these near relations represent such as by notions and external observances deceive themselves, and such as more grossly attempt to impose upon others. They are both actuated by vain glory, and seek the applause of men in their religious profession and most zealous performances; while the credit thus acquired subserves also their temporal interest: but repentance, conversion, and the life of faith, would not only cost them too much labor, but destroy the very principle by which they are actuated. By a much 'shorter cut,' they become a part of the visible church, are satisfied with a form of godliness, and kept in countenance by great numbers among every description of professing Christians, and the example of multitudes in every age. Their confidence, however, will not bear the light of Scripture; they therefore shrink from investigation, and treat with derision and reproaches all who would convince them of their fatal mistake, or show them the real nature of evangelical religion.

I saw that they all went on, save that Christian kept before, who had no more talk but with himself, and that

sometimes sighingly, and sometimes comfortably.—Even such Christians as are most assured of their acceptance, and competent to perceive the awful delusions of false professors, find cause for sighs amidst their comforts, when employed in serious retired self-reflection. Nothing can exclude the uneasiness which arises from indwelling sin, with its unavoidable effects, and from the crimes and miseries they witness around them.

CHAPTER VII

THE HILL DIFFICULTY

They all went on till they came to the foot of the hill Difficulty.—The hill Difficulty represents those circumstances which require peculiar self-denial and exertion, that commonly prove the believer's sincerity, after he has first obtained 'a good hope through grace.' The opposition of the world, the renunciation of temporal interests, or the painful task of overcoming inveterate evil habits or constitutional propensities (which during his first anxious earnestness seemed perhaps to be destroyed, though in fact they were only suspended:) these and such like trials prove a severe test; but there is no hope, except in pressing forward; and the encouragements, received under the faithful ministry of the Gospel, prepare the soul for every conflict and effort. There are, however, by-ways; and the difficulty may be avoided without a man's renouncing his profession: he may decline the self-denying duty, or refuse the demanded sacrifice, and find some plausible excuse to his own conscience, or among his neighbors. But the true believer will be suspicious of these easier ways, on the right hand or the left: his path lies straight forward, and cannot be travelled without ascending the hill: which he desires to do, because his grand concern is to be found right at last. On the contrary, they who chiefly desire, at a cheap rate, to keep up their credit and confidence, will venture into perilous or ruinous paths, till they either openly apostatize, or get entangled in some fatal delusion, and are heard of no more among the people of God. These lines are here inserted—

'Shall they who wrong begin yet rightly end?
Shall they at all have safety for their friend?
No, no; in headstrong manner they set out,
And headlong they will fall at last, no doubt.'

He fell from running to going, and from going to clambering upon his hands and his knees, because of the steepness of the place.—The difficulties of believers often seem to increase as they proceed; this damps their spirits, and they find more painful exertion requisite in pressing forward, than they expected, especially when they were rejoicing in the Lord: he however helps them, and provides for their refreshment, that they may not faint. But, whether their trials be moderated, or remarkable divine consolations be vouchsafed, it is, alas! very common for them to presume too much on their perseverance hitherto, and on the privileges to which they have been admitted: thus their ardor abates, their diligence and vigilance are relaxed, and they venture to allow themselves some respite from exertion. Then drowsiness steals upon them, darkness envelopes their souls, the evidences of their acceptance are obscured or lost, and the event would be fatal, did not the Lord excite them to renewed earnestness by salutary warnings and alarms. Nor are believers at any time more exposed to this temptation, than when outward ease has succeeded to great hardships, patiently and conscientiously endured; for at such a crisis they are least disposed to question their own sincerity; and Satan is sure to employ all his subtlety to lull them into such a security as is in fact an abuse of the Lord's special goodness vouchsafed to them.

The farther we go, the more danger we meet with, wherefore we turned, and are going back again.—Some persons are better prepared to struggle through difficulties, than to face dangers; alarming convictions will induce them to exercise a temporary self-denial, and to exert themselves with diligence; yet the very appearance of persecution will drive them back to their forsaken courses and companions. Through unbelief, distrust, and timidity, they fear the rage of men more than the wrath of God; and never consider how easily the Lord can restrain or disarm the fiercest persecutors. Even true Christians are sometimes alarmed by the discourse of such persons; but, as they believe the word of God, they are 'moved by fear' to go forward at all hazards: such terrors, as induce mere professors to apostasy, excite upright souls to renewed self-examination by the Holy Scriptures, that they may 'rejoice in hope' amidst their perils and tribulations; and this often tends to discover to them those decays and losses, in respect of the vigor of holy affection, and the evidences of their acceptance, which had before escaped their notice. Christian's perplexity, fear, sorrow, remorse, redoubled earnestness, complaints, and self-reproachings, when he missed his roll, and went back to seek it, exactly suit the experience of humble and conscientious believers, when unwatchfulness has brought their state into uncertainty; but they do not at all accord to that of professors, who strive against all doubts indiscriminately, more than against any sin whatever, which is not connected with open scandal; who strive hard to keep up their confidence against evidence, amidst continued negligence and allowed sins; and exclaim against sighs, tears, and tenderness of conscience, as legality and unbelief. Bunyan would have excluded such professors from the company of his pilgrims, though they often pass muster in modern times.

Now by this time he was come to the arbor again, where for a while he sat down and wept.—By means of extraordinary diligence, with renewed application to the blood of Christ, the believer will in time recover his warranted confidence, and God will 'restore to him the joy of his salvation:' but he must, as it were, pass repeatedly over the same ground with sorrow, which, had it not been for his negligence, he might have passed at once with comfort.

Instead of the words, 'as God would have it,' all the old copies read, 'as Christian would have it;' which must mean, that the Lord fully granted his desires. But modern editors have substituted, 'as Providence would have it,' which is indeed clear sense, but not much in our author's manner, who perhaps would rather have ascribed Christian's success to special grace; yet, as some mistake seems to have crept into the old editions, I have ventured my conjecture in the emendation of it, of which the reader may judge for himself.

The sun went down upon Christian; this made him again recall the vanity of his sleeping to his remembrance; and thus he again began to condole with himself.—Believers may recover their evidences of acceptance, and yet suffer many troubles as the effects of their past unwatchfulness. The Lord rebukes and chastens those whom he loves: genuine comfort springs immediately from the vigorous exercise of holy affections in communion with God, which may be suspended even when no doubts are entertained of final salvation; and the true penitent is least disposed to forgive himself, when most satisfied that the Lord hath forgiven him.

Behold there was a very stately palace before him, the name of which was Beautiful, and it stood by the highway-side.—Hitherto Christian had been a solitary pilgrim; but we must next consider him as admitted to the communion of the faithful, and joining with them in the most solemn public ordinances. This is represented under the emblem of the house Beautiful, and the pilgrim's entertainment in it.

CHAPTER VIII

THE PALACE BEAUTIFUL

Looking very narrowly before him as he went, he espied two lions in the way.—A public profession of faith exposes a man to more opposition from relatives and neighbors than a private attention to religion; and in our author's days, it was commonly the signal for persecution; for which reason he places the lions in the road to the house Beautiful. Sense perceives the danger to which an open profession of religion may expose a man, and the imagination through the suggestions of Satan, exceedingly magnifies them; faith alone can discern the secret restraints which the Lord lays on the minds of opposers; and even believers are apt to be fearful and distrustful on such occasions. But the vigilant pastors of the flock obviate their fears, and by seasonable admonitions animate them to press forward, assured that nothing shall do them any real harm, and that all shall eventually prove beneficial to them. We meet with the following lines in the old copies, which, though misplaced in most of them, may refer to the pilgrim's present situation.

> 'Difficulty is behind, fear is before,
> Though he's got on the hill, the lions roar:
> A Christian man is never long at ease;
> When one fright's gone, another doth him seize.'

The Porter also asked whence he was, and whither he was going?—The porter's inquiries and Christian's answers exhibit our author's sentiments on the caution with which members should be admitted into the communion of the faithful;

and it very properly shows, how ministers, by private conversation, may form a judgment of a man's profession, whether it be intelligent and the result of experience, or notional and formal. Christian assigned his sinful sleeping as the cause of his arriving so late: when believers are oppressed with prevailing doubts of their acceptance, they are backward in joining themselves to God's people; and this often tempts them to sinful delays, instead of exciting them to greater diligence. The subsequent discourse of Discretion with the pilgrim represents such precautions and inquiries into the character and views of a professor, as may be made use of by any body of Christians, in order to prevent the intrusion of improper persons. The answers, given to the several questions proposed, constitute the proper external qualifications for admission to the Lord's table, when there is nothing in a man's principles and conduct inconsistent with them: the Lord alone can judge how far they accord to the inward dispositions and affections of the heart. By the little discourse of others belonging to the family with Christian previous to his admission, the author probably meant, that members should be admitted into Christian societies with the approbation, at least, of the most prudent, pious, and candid part of those that constitute them; and according to the dictates of those graces or endowments here personified. By giving him 'something to eat before supper,' he probably referred to those preparatory sermons and devotions, by which the administration of the Lord's supper was then frequently and with great propriety introduced.

Piety: Come, good Christian, since we have been so loving to you to receive you into our house this night.— The further conversation of Piety and her companions with Christian, was subsequent to his admission, and represents the advantage of the communion of the saints, and the best method of conducting it. To lead believers to a serious review of the way in which they have been led hitherto is every way profitable, as it tends to increase humiliation, gratitude, faith, and hope; and must, therefore, proportionably conduce to the glory of God, and the edification of their brethren.

Then Prudence thought good to ask him a few questions, and desired his answer to them.—Men may learn by human teaching to profess any doctrine, and relate any experience; nay, general convictions, transient affections, and distinct notions may impose upon the man himself, and he may mistake them for true conversion. The best method of avoiding this dangerous rock consists in daily self-examination, and constant prayer to be preserved from it; and, as far as we are concerned, to form a judgment of others, in order to perform our several duties towards them, prudence is especially required, and will suggest such questions as follow in this place. The true Christian's inmost feelings will best explain the answers, which no exposition can elucidate to those who are unacquainted with the conflict to which they refer. The golden hours (fleeting and precious) are earnests of the everlasting holy felicity of heaven.

Then said Charity to Christian, Have you a family? are you a married man?—When a man knows the value of his own soul, he will become greatly solicitous for the souls of others. It is, therefore, a very suspicious circumstance, when a professor shows no earnestness in persuading those he loves best to seek salvation also; and it is absurd to excuse this negligence by arguments taken from God's secret purposes, when these have no influence on the conduct of the same persons in their temporal concerns. Charity's discourse with Christian shows what our author thought to be the duties of believers in this most important concern, and what he understood to be the real reasons why carnal men reject the Gospel.

Thus they sat talking together until supper was ready.—The administration of the Lord's supper is here emblematically described. In it the person, humiliation, sufferings, and death of Christ, with the motive and event of them, are kept in perpetual remembrance. By seriously contemplating these interesting subjects, with the emblems of his body wounded, and his blood shed, before our eyes; and by professing our cordial acceptance of his purchased salvation, and surrender of ourselves to his service, we find every holy affection revived and invigorated, and our souls melted into deep repentance, inspired with calm confidence, animated to thankful, zealous, self-denying obedience, and softened into tender affection for our fellow Christians, with compassionate forgiving love of our most inveterate enemies. The believer will readily apply the allegorical representation of 'the Lord of the hill' (Isaiah 25:6, 7) to the love of Christ for lost sinners, which no words can adequately describe, for it 'passeth knowledge.'

The pilgrim they laid in a large upper chamber,

whose window opened towards the sun-rising: the name of the chamber was Peace.—That peace of conscience and serenity of mind, which follow an humble upright profession of faith in Christ, and communion with him and his people, is not the effect of a mere outward observance; but of that inward disposition of the heart which is thus cultivated, and of the Lord's blessing on his own appointments. This is here represented by the chamber Peace: it raises the soul above the care and bustle of this vain world, and springs from the healing beams of the Sun of righteousness.

First they had him into the study, where they showed him records of the greatest antiquity.—Christian communion, properly conducted, tends to enlarge the believer's acquaintance with the Holy Scriptures: and this conduces to the increase of faith, hope, love, patience, and fortitude; to animate the soul in emulating the illustrious examples there exhibited, and to furnish instruction for every good work.

The next day they took him, and had him into the armory, where they showed him all manner of furniture.—The provision, which is made in Christ and his fullness, for maintaining and increasing, in the hearts of his people, those holy dispositions and affections, by the vigorous exercise of which victory is obtained over all their enemies, is here represented by the armory (Ephesians 6:10–18; 1 Thessalonians 5:6). This suffices for all who seek to be supplied from it, how many soever they be. We ought, therefore, 'to take to ourselves the whole armor of God,' and 'put it on,' by diligently using all the means of grace; and we may assist others, by our exhortations, counsels, example, and prayers, in doing the same. The following allusions to the Scripture history, which have a peculiar propriety in an allegory, intimate, that the means of grace are made effectual by the power of God, which we should depend on, in implicit obedience to his appointments.

We will, if the day be clear, show you the Delectable Mountains.—The Delectable Mountains, as seen at a distance, represent those distinct views of the privileges and consolations attainable in this life, with which believers are sometimes favored, when attending on divine ordinances, or diligently making a subsequent improvement of them. The hopes thus inspired prepare them for meeting and pressing forward through dangers and hardships; this is the pre-eminent advantage of Christian communion, and can only be enjoyed at some special seasons, when the Sun of righteousness shines upon the soul.

Now he bethought himself of setting forward, and they were willing he should.—The ordinances of public or social worship are only the means of being religious, not the essence of religion itself. Having renewed our strength by waiting on the Lord, we must go forward, by attending with increasing diligence to the duties of our several stations, and preparing to resist temptations, which often assault us after special seasons of divine consolation. Ministers, therefore, and experienced believers should warn young converts to expect trials and conflicts, and recommend to them such companions as may be a comfort and help in their pilgrimage.

Then he began to go forward; but Discretion, Piety, Charity, and Prudence would accompany him down to the foot of the hill.—The humiliation requisite for receiving Christ, obtaining peace, and making a good confession of the faith, is general and indistinct, compared with that which subsequent trials and conflicts will produce; and the Lord commonly dispenses comfort and humiliating experiences alternately, that the believer may neither be elated nor depressed above measure (2 Corinthians 12:1–5); the valley of Humiliation, therefore, is very judiciously placed beyond the house Beautiful. Some explain it to signify a Christian's outward circumstances, when reduced to poverty, or subjected to great temporal loss by professing the Gospel; and perhaps the author had this idea in his mind; yet it could only be viewed as the means of producing inward humiliation. In going down into the valley, the believer will greatly need the assistance of discretion, piety, charity, and prudence, and the recollection of the instructions and counsels of such Christians as are eminent for these endowments: for humiliating dispensations and experiences excite the latent evils of the heart, and often cause men to speak and act unadvisedly; so that, notwithstanding every precaution, the review will commonly discover many things, which demand the remorse and sorrow of deep repentance.

CHAPTER IX

APOLLYON

He espied a foul fiend coming over the field to meet him: his name is Apollyon.—Under discouraging circumstances the believer will often be tempted to murmur, despond, or seek relief from the world. Finding that his two sanguine expectations are not answered, that he grows worse rather than better in his own opinion of himself, that his comforts are transitory, and that much reproach, contempt, and loss, are incurred by his profession of religion, discontent will often rise up in his heart, and weakness of faith will expose him to sharp conflicts. Mr. Bunyan, having experienced, in an uncommon degree, the most dreadful temptations, was probably led by that circumstance to speak on this subject in language not very intelligible to those who have been exempted from such painful exercises of mind. The nature of his work required, that they should be described under outward emblems; but the inward suggestions of evil spirits are especially intended. These seem to have peculiar access to the imagination, and are able to paint before that illusive faculty the most alluring or terrifying representations, as if they were realities. Apollyon signifies the destroyer (Revelation 9:11;) and in carrying on the work of destruction, fallen angels endeavor by various devices to deter men from prayer, and to render them afraid of those things, without which the life of faith cannot be maintained; in order that after convictions, they may be led to give up religion, as the only method of recovering composure of mind. Many, 'having no root in themselves,' thus gradually fall away; and others are greatly retarded: but the well instructed believer sees no safety, except in facing his enemy. If there appears to be danger, in persevering, ruin is inevitable if he desist (for Christian 'had no armor for his back;') even fear, therefore, will in that case induce a man to stand his ground, and the more resolutely he resists temptation, the sooner will he regain his tranquillity: for when the suggestions of Satan excite us to pray more fervently, and to be more diligent in every service, that enemy will 'flee from us.' Perhaps some may remember a time when they were so harassed as almost to despair of relief; who have since been so entirely delivered, that, were it not for the recollection of their own past experience, they would be ready to ascribe all such things to disease or enthusiasm, notwithstanding all that the Scripture contains on the subject.

He had wings like a dragon, feet like a bear, and out of his belly came fire and smoke, and his mouth was as the mouth of a lion.—The description of Apollyon implies, that the combat afterwards recorded particularly represented the terrors by which evil spirits attempt to drive professors out of their path. Other temptations, though perhaps more dangerous, are not so distressing: 'Satan can transform himself into an angel of light;' and indeed he is a very Proteus, who can assume any form, as best suits his purpose. As all have been overcome by the temptations of the devil, and 'of whom a man is overcome, of the same is he brought into bondage;' so by usurpation, he is become the god and prince of this world, and we have all been his slaves. But believers, having been redeemed by the blood of Christ, 'are made free from sin and become the servants of God:' and the abiding conviction, that all the subjects of sin and Satan must perish, concurs with their experience of its hard bondage, in fortifying them against every temptation to return to it. Sensible of their obligations to God as their Creator and Governor, they have deeply repented of their past rebellions; and having obtained mercy, feel themselves bound by gratitude and the most solemn engagements to cleave to him and his service. Their difficulties and discouragements cannot induce them to believe that they 'have changed for the worse;' nor will they be influenced by the numbers who apostatize, from love to the world and dread of the cross; for they are 'rooted and grounded in love,' and not merely moved by fears and hopes. They are sure that the Lord is able to deliver them from their enemies; and should the wicked be permitted to prosper in their malicious devices, they know enough of his plan, to rely on his wisdom, truth, and love in the midst of sufferings. Thus they have answers ready for every suggestion; even such answers as Christian had been furnished with at the house of the Interpreter. If such temptations prove ineffectual, Satan will perhaps assault the believer, by representing to his mind, with every possible aggravation, the several instances of his misconduct, since he professed the Gospel, in order to heighten his apprehensions of being found at last a hypocrite: when the soul is discouraged and gloomy, he will be as assiduous in representing every false step to be a horrid crime inconsistent with a state of grace, as he is at other times in persuading men, that the most flagrant violations of the Divine law are mere trifles. In repelling such suggestions, the well-instructed believer will neither deny the charge, nor extenuate his guilt; but he will flee for refuge to the free grace of the Gospel, and take comfort from the consciousness that he now hates, and groans under the remains of those evils, which once he wholly lived in without remorse; thence inferring, that 'his sins though many, are forgiven.'

Then Apollyon broke out into a grievous rage, saying, I am an enemy to this Prince.—Thus far Christian's contest with Apollyon is intelligible and instructive to every experienced believer: what follows is more difficult. But if we duly reflect upon the Lord's permission to Satan, in respect of Job, with the efforts and effects that followed; and if we compare it with the tempter's desire of sifting Peter and the other apostles as wheat—we shall not be greatly at a loss about our author's meaning. This enemy is sometimes gratified with such an arrangement of outward dispensations as most favors his assaults: so that the believer's path seems to be wholly obstructed. The Lord himself appears to have forsaken him, or even to fight against him; and his appointments are deemed contrary to his promises. This gives Satan an opportunity of suggesting hard thoughts of God and his ways, doubts about the truth of the Scriptures, and desponding fears of a fatal event to a self-denying course of religion. Many such 'fiery darts' may be repelled or quenched by the shield of faith; but there are seasons (as some of us well know) when they are poured in so incessantly, and receive such plausibility from facts, and when they so interrupt a man while praying, reading, or meditating,

that he is tempted to intermit religious duties, to avoid their
horrid concomitants. The evils of the heart, which seemed
before to be subdued, are at these times so excited by means of
the imagination, that they apparently prevail more than ever,
rendering every service an abomination, as well as a burden; so
that the harassed soul, alarmed, baffled, defiled, self-detested,
and thinking that God and his servants unite in abhorring
him, is ready to give up all hope, to doubt all his former principles, to seek refuge in some heretical or antinomian system,
or to attempt the dissipation of his melancholy gloom, by joining again in the vanities of the world. Thus the enemy 'wounds
him in his understanding, faith, and conversation,' (according
to the author's marginal interpretation of his meaning,) yet he
cannot find relief in this manner; but is inwardly constrained,
with renewed efforts, to return to the conflict. But when such
temptations are long continued, resistance will gradually
become more feeble; the distressed believer will be ready to
give up every thing; and when the enemy plies him closely with
infidel suggestions, to which his circumstances give a specious
occasion, he may be thrown down, and 'his sword may fly out of
his hand:' so that for a time he may be unable to give any credit
to the truth of the Scriptures, by which alone he was before
enabled to repel the tempter. This is a dreadful case: and could
true faith thus finally and entirely fail, even real Christians
must perish. Satan hath succeeded against many professors,
with half these advantages; and he may be supposed at least,
to boast that he is sure of such as are thus cast down. But the
advocate above 'prays' for his disciples, 'that their faith should
not fail' (Luke 22:31, 32). So that, though Peter fell with Judas,
he was not left to perish with him. The Christian, therefore,
though 'almost pressed to death,' and ready 'to despair of life,'
will, by the special grace of God, be helped again to seize his
sword, and to use it with more effect than ever. The Holy Spirit
will bring to his mind, with the most convincing energy, the
evidences of the divine inspiration of the Scripture, and enable
him to rely on the promises: and thus, at length, the enemy
will be put to flight, by testimonies of holy writ pertinently
adduced, and more clearly understood than before. Experience
will teach some readers to understand these things, and they
will know how to compassionate and make allowances for the
mistakes of the tempted: and others, who have been graciously

exempted from, perhaps, the deepest anguish known on earth (though commonly not of long duration), should learn from the testimony of their brethren, to allow the reality of these distresses, and sympathize with the sufferers; and not (like Job's friends) to join with Satan in aggravating their sorrows. We may allow, that constitution, partial disease, and errors in judgment, expose some men more than others to such assaults; yet these are only occasions, and evil spirits are assuredly the agents in thus harassing serious persons. It is indeed of the greatest importance to be well established in the faith: they, who in ordinary cases are satisfied with general convictions and comfortable feelings, without being able to give a reason for their hope, may be driven to the most tremendous extremities, should God permit them to be thus assaulted: for they have no fixed principles to which they may resort in such an emergency; and perhaps some degree of mistake always gives Satan his principal advantage on these occasions. Yet men of the most sober minds and sound judgment, when in a better state of bodily health than usual, and in all other respects more rational, have experienced such distressing temptations of this kind, as they could scarcely have believed on the report of others; and when delivered, they cannot look back on the past without the greatest consternation. Besides the verses, by which Christian gave thanks to his great deliverer, we meet in the old copies with these lines:—

> 'A more unequal match can hardly be,
> Christian must fight an angel; but you see,
> The valiant man by handling sword and shield,
> Doth make him, though a dragon, quit the field.'

There came to him a hand with some of the leaves of the tree of life, the which Christian took and applied to the wounds that he had received in the battle, and was healed immediately.—When the believer has obtained the victory over temptation, the Lord will graciously heal all the wounds he received in the conflict; pardoning his sins, rectifying his mistakes, and renewing his strength and comfort, through the mediation of Christ, and by the influences of the Holy Spirit: so that the most distressing experiences are often succeeded by the sweetest confidence and serenity of mind, and the greatest alacrity in the ways of God. 'The leaves of the tree of life' (Revelation 22:2,) represent the present benefits of the redemption of Christ: 'the hand' may be the emblem of those whom the Lord employs, as instruments in restoring to his discouraged servants 'the joy of his salvation.' The believer thus healed and refreshed, by meditation on the death of Christ, and other religious exercises, rests not in one victory, but presses forward, prepared for new conflicts; yet the enemy, once decidedly put to flight, seldom repeats the same assaults, at least for some time; because he will generally find the victor upon his guard on that side, though he may be surprised in some other way.

CHAPTER X

THE VALLEY OF THE SHADOW OF DEATH

***Now, at the end of this valley was another, called the
Valley of the Shadow of Death.***—The Valley of the Shadow
of Death seems intended to represent a variation of inward distress, conflict, and alarm, which arises from prevailing darkness and insensibility of mind, rendering a man reluctant to
religious duties, and dull in the performance of them, which
makes way for manifold apprehensions and temptations. The
words, quoted from the prophet, describe the waste howling
wilderness through which Israel journeyed to Canaan; which
typified the believer's pilgrimage through this world to heaven.
From this we may infer, that the author meant in general, that
such dreary seasons may be expected, as very few believers
wholly escape them: but we must not suppose, that he intended
to convey an idea, that all experience these trials in the same
order or degree as Christian did. While men rest in forms and
notions, they generally expect nothing in religious ordinances
but to finish a task, and to enjoy the satisfaction of having
done their supposed duty; but the spiritual worshipper, at
some times, finds his soul filled with clear light and holy affection; 'it is good for him to draw nigh to God;' and 'his soul is
satisfied with marrow and fatness, while he praises his God
with joyful lips:' at other times, dulness and heaviness oppress
him; he feels little exercise of faith, hope, desire, reverence,
love, or gratitude; he seems to address an unknown or absent
God, and rather to mock than to worship him; divine things
appear obscure and almost unreal; and every returning season of devotion, or reiterated effort to lift up his heart to God,

ends in disappointment; so that religion becomes his burden instead of delight. Evils before unnoticed are now perceived to mingle with his services; for his self-knowledge is advanced; his remedy seems to increase his disease; he suspects that all his former joy was a delusion, and is ready to conclude, that 'God hath forgotten to be gracious, and hath shut up his loving-kindness in displeasure.' These experiences, sufficiently painful in themselves, are often rendered more distressing, by erroneous expectations of uninterrupted comfort, or by reading books, or hearkening to instructions, which state things unscripturally; representing comfort as the evidence of acceptance, assurance as the essence of faith, impressions or visions as the witness of the Spirit; or perfection as attainable in this life, nay, actually attained by all the regenerate; as if this were the church triumphant, and not the church militant. The state of the body also, as disordered by nervous or hypochondriacal affections, gives energy to the distressing inferences which men often draw from their dark frame of mind; and indeed indisposition may often operate as a direct cause of it; though the influences of the Holy Spirit will overcome this, and all other impediments to comfort, when 'he sheds abroad the love of God in the heart.' Evil spirits never fail, when permitted, to take advantage of a disordered state, whether of body or mind, to mislead, entangle, perplex, or defile the soul. Persons of a melancholic temperament, when not aware of the particular causes whence their gloom originates, are apt to ascribe it wholly to desertion, which exceedingly enhances their distress; and, as our author had been greatly harassed in this way, he has given us a larger proportion of this shade than is generally met with by consistent believers, or than the Scriptures give us reason to expect: and probably he meant to state the outlines of his own experience in the pilgrimage of Christian.

When Christian was got to the borders of the Shadow of Death, there met him two men.—These men were spies, not pilgrims; they related what they had observed at a distance, but had never experienced. They represent those who have been conversant with godly people; and 'bring an evil report on the good land,' to prejudice the minds of numbers against the right ways of the Lord. Such men pretend to have made trial of religion, and found it to be a comfortless and dreary pursuit; they give a caricatured description of the sighs, groans, terrors, and distresses of pious persons, and of all the dreadful things to be seen and heard among them: they avail themselves of every unguarded or hyperbolical expression, which escapes a tempted believer; of the enthusiastic representations which some people give of their experience; and even of the figurative language, which is often employed in speaking of inward conflicts under images taken from external things. Thus they endeavor to excuse their own apostasy, and to expose to contempt the cause which they have deserted. Nothing they can say, however, concerning the disorder or confusion to which religion may sometimes give occasion, can induce the believer to conclude that he has mistaken his way, or that it would be advisable for him to turn back, or deviate into any by-path: though they will excite him to vigilance and circumspection. As those spies do so much mischief by their misrepresentations, we should be careful to give them as little occasion as we possibly can.

So far as this valley reached, there was on the right hand a very deep ditch; that ditch is it into which the blind have led the blind in all ages.—The fatal presumption, into which men are soothed, through ignorance and various kinds of false doctrine, so that they conclude themselves safe without any warrant from Scripture, is intended by the 'deep ditch,' into which the blind lead the blind and perish with them. This is often done by men who reciprocally criminate and despise each other. 'The dangerous quag,' on the other side of the narrow way, represents the opposite extreme—despair of God's mercy; and the mire of it agrees with that of the Slough of Despond. In these opposite ways multitudes continually perish; some concluding that there is no fear, others that there is no hope. But the danger to which a real believer is exposed, of verging towards one of these extremes in times of inward darkness and disconsolation, is especially implied. They, who have had much opportunity of conversing with professors of the Gospel, have met with many persons who once were zealous and comfortable, but their religious affections have declined; their duties are comparatively scanty, formal, and joyless; their walk unsteady, and their hearts dark, cold, and barren; they call themselves backsliders and complain of desertion, yet they have no hearts to use proper means of revival, but love to be soothed in their present condition; and quiet themselves by presuming that they are true believers, and abusing the doctrine of final perseverance. Many of this cast are wholly deceived; others partially, and will be recovered by severe but salutary discipline. Even the true Christian, when greatly discouraged, may be powerfully tempted to seek peace of mind, by arguing with himself on the safety of his state, or trying to be satisfied without his former spiritual affections and holy consolations: and Satan will find prompters to suggest to him, that this is the case of all experienced believers, and that fervency of love belongs only to young converts, who are strangers to their own hearts. This is the more plausible, because the increase of sound judgment and abiding spiritual affections abates that earnestness (often indiscreet and disproportioned,) which sprang from mere selfish principles: and, when religious profession is cheap and common, many retain it, who have scarce any appearance of spirituality, and who infect others with their contagious converse and example. But while the conscientious believer, amidst his deepest discouragements, dreads and shuns this presumption, he is liable to sink into despondency; and may be led to condemn all his past experience as unreal; to rank himself among stony-ground hearers; to conclude that it is useless for him to pray or seek any more; and to lie down in enfeebling dejection. Again, perceiving this danger, he finds it very difficult, in the present dark state of his soul, to avoid it, without seeming to abuse the free grace of the gospel. This experience must create much distress, perplexity, and confusion; and makes way for many dark and terrifying temptations; so that, though a man be not harassed with doubts about the truth of the Scriptures, he will be unable to make much use of them for his direction and comfort; and earnest, instant prayer must be his only resource. Cases sometimes occur, in which, through a concurrence of circumstances, this alarming and perplexing experience continues and increases for some time: but the true Christian will be, as it were, constrained to press forward, and by faith will at length put his enemies to flight. Some have thought, that the general notions of apparitions may be alluded to, as giving the tempter an occasion of increasing the terror of such persons as are in that respect credulous and timorous.

One thing I would not let slip: I took notice, that now poor Christian was so confounded, that he did not

know his own voice.—The case here intended is not uncommon among conscientious persons under urgent temptations. Imaginations are suddenly excited in their minds, with which their previous thoughts had no connection, even as if words were spoken to them: these often imply hard censures of God, his service or decrees, which they abhor as direct blasphemy; or harass them with other hateful ideas: yet, instead of considering, that such suggestions distress them, in exact proportion as they are opposite to the prevailing disposition of their hearts, and that their dread and hatred of them are evidences of love to God, they consider them as unpardonably criminal, inconsistent with a state of grace; and a mark of final reprobation. Whereas, had such things coincided with the state of their minds, they would have been defiling but not distressing; and instead of rejecting them at once with decided abhorrence, they would have given them entertainment, and employed their minds about them, as much as they dared: 'for the carnal mind is enmity against God,' and can only be deterred from blasphemy, on many occasions, by the dread of his vengeance. Our author had been so much baffled by this stratagem of the tempter, that it would have been extraordinary had he omitted it: for the subsequent discovery he made of his mistake, and of the way of resisting the devil in this case, qualified him to give suitable caution to others. The intrusion of such thoughts should excite us to greater earnestness in prayer, pious meditations, or adoring praises; for this, above all other things, will in the event be found to close the mind most effectually against them. The following lines come in here, as before—

> 'Poor man! where art thou now? thy day is night:
> Good man, be not cast down, thou yet art right.
> The way to heaven lies by the gates of hell:
> Cheer up, hold out, with thee it shall go well.'

When Christian had travelled in this disconsolate condition some considerable time, he thought he heard the voice of a man, as going before him.—Nothing more effectually supports the tempted than to learn, that others, whom they consider as believers, have been or are in similar circumstances: for the idea, that such a state of mind as they experience is inconsistent with true faith, gives the enemy his principal advantage against them. Indeed this often proves the means of their deliverance; for in due season that light, affection, and consolation, for which they have long mourned, thirsted, prayed, and waited, will be vouchsafed them; and the review of the dangers they have escaped, now more clearly discerned than before, will enlarge their hearts with admiring gratitude to their great and gracious deliverer.

Though the first part of the Valley of the Shadow of Death was dangerous, yet this second part, which he was yet to go, was, if possible, far more dangerous.—Various interpretations are given of this second part of the valley, which only show, that the author's precise idea in it lies more remote from general apprehension than in other passages: for they all coincide with some of the difficulties or dangers that are clearly described under other emblems. I would not indeed be too confident, but, I apprehend, in general we are taught by it, that believers are not most in danger when under the deepest distress; that the snares and devices of the enemy are so many and various, through the several stages of our pilgrimage, as to baffle all description or enumeration; and that all the emblems of the valley of humiliation, and of the shadow of death, could not fully represent the thousandth part of them. Were it not, therefore, that the Lord undertakes to guide his people, by the light of his word and Spirit, they never could possibly escape them all.

CHAPTER XI

CHRISTIAN AND FAITHFUL

As Christian went on his way, he came to a little ascent, which was cast up on purpose that pilgrims might see before them.—This may represent those moments of encouragement, in which tempted believers rise superior to their difficulties; and are animated to desire the company of their brethren, whom dejection under humiliating experience disposes them to shun. The conduct of Christian intimates, that believers are sometimes ready to hinder one another, by making their own attainments and progress a standard for their brethren; but the lively exercise of faith renders men intent on pressing forward, and more apt to fear the society of such as would influence them to loiter, than to stop for them. This tends to excite an useful emulation; but while it promotes diligence, it often gives occasion to those risings of vain glory and self-preference, which are the forerunners of some humiliating fall: thus believers often are left to feel their need of help from the very persons whom they have foolishly undervalued. Such experiences, however, give occasion to those mutual good offices, which unite them more closely in the nearest ties of tender affection.

Christian: My honored and well-beloved brother Faithful, I am glad that I have overtaken you.—This episode, so to speak, with others of the same kind, gives our author a happy advantage of varying the characters and experiences of Christians, as found in real life; and of thus avoiding the common fault of making one man a standard for others, in the circumstances of his religious progress. It often happens, that they who have been acquainted before their conversion, and hear little of each other for some time after, find at length that they were led to attend to religion about the same period, without having opportunity or courage to confer together about it. The decided separation of a sinner from his old companions, and his avowed dread of the wrath to come, frequently excites alarms and serious thoughts in the minds of others, which they are not able wholly to shake off. In many indeed this is a mere floating, transient notion, insufficient to overcome the propensities of the carnal mind; but when it arises from a real belief of God's testimony it will at length produce a happy change.

He is now seven times worse than if he had never gone out of the city.—Apostates are often ashamed to own they have had convictions: their careless companions assume a kind of superiority over them; they do not think them hearty in the cause of ungodliness, and they despise their cowardice and versatility: on the other hand such persons feel that they want an apology, and have recourse to contemptible lies and slanders, with abject servility; while they shun religious people, as afraid of their arguments, warnings, and expostulations.

Faithful: I escaped the slough that I perceived you fell into, and got up to the gate without that danger.—Some men are preserved from desponding fears, and the suggestions of worldly wisdom, by receiving more distinct views of the general truths of the Gospel; and thus they proceed with less hesitation and interruption in applying to Christ for salvation: yet, perhaps, their temperature, turn of mind, habits of life, and peculiar situation, render them more accessible to temptations of another kind; and they may be more in danger from the fascinations of fleshly lusts. Thus in different ways the Lord makes his people sensible of their depravity, weakness, and exposed situation; while he so moderates the temptation, or interposes for their deliverance, that they are preserved, and taught to ascribe all the glory to his name.

Faithful: Why, at first I found myself somewhat inclinable to go with the man, for I thought he spoke very fair.— Those Christians, who by strong faith or assured hope, endure hardships more cheerfully than their brethren, are often exposed to greater danger from the allurements of outward objects, exciting the remaining propensities of corrupt nature. Deep humiliation and great anxiety about the event, in many instances, tend to repress the lusts of the heart, by supplying a continual succession of other thoughts and cares: while constant encouragement, readily attained, too often leaves a man to experience them more forcibly. Nay, the same persons, who under pressing solicitude seem to be entirely delivered from some peculiar corruptions, find them revive and become very troublesome, when they have obtained more confidence about their salvation. The old Adam, the corrupt nature, proves a constant snare to many believers, by its hankering after the pleasures, riches, honors, and pride of the world; nor can the victory be secured without great difficulty and trouble, and strong faith and fervent prayer.

Christian: That man that overtook you was Moses.— The doctrine of Moses did not essentially differ from that of Christ: but the giving of the law, that ministration of condemnation to all sinners, formed so prominent a part of his dispensation, in which the Gospel was exhibited under types and shadows, that 'the law' is said to have been 'given by Moses,' while 'grace and truth came by Jesus Christ;' especially as the shadows were of no further use when the substance was come. Even such hankerings after worldly objects, are as effectually opposed and repressed, being contrary to the spirituality of the precept, 'Thou shalt not covet,' often greatly discourage the new convert; who does not duly recollect, that the Gospel brings relief to those who feel themselves justly condemned by the law. Yet these terrors produce deeper humiliation, and greater simplicity of dependence on the mercy of God in Christ Jesus, as 'the end of the law for righteousness to every one that believeth.' Many for a time escape discouragement, because they are but superficially acquainted with their own hearts; yet it is proper they should be further instructed by such experiences as are here described, in order to their greater stability, tenderness of conscience, and compassion for their brethren, in the subsequent part of their pilgrimage.

Because I had so much of the day before me, I passed by the Porter, and came down the hill.—This circumstance seems to imply, that, in our author's judgment, even eminent believers sometimes decline entering into communion with their brethren according to his views of it; and that very lively affections and strong consolations may probably have rendered them less attentive to these externals. Indeed he deemed this a disadvantage and a mistake (which is perhaps also intimated by Faithful's not calling at the house of the Interpreter), but not a sufficient reason why other Christians should not cordially unite with them. This is a beautiful example of that candor, in respect of those things about which pious persons differ, that consists with decided firmness in the great essentials of faith and holiness.

Faithful: Yes, I met with one Discontent, who would willingly have persuaded me to go back again with him.—While some believers are most tried with inward fears and conflicts, others are more tempted to repine at the outward degradation, reproach, ridicule, and loss to which religion exposes them. A man, perhaps, at first, may flatter himself with the hope of avoiding the peculiarities and eccentricities, which have brought enmity or contempt on some professors of the Gospel; and of ensuring respect and affection, by caution, uprightness, and benevolence; but further experience and knowledge constrain him to adopt and avow sentiments, and associate with persons, that the world despises; and, seeing himself invincibly impelled by his conscience, to a line of conduct which ensures the reproach of enthusiasm and folly, the loss of friends, and manifold mortifications, he is powerfully assaulted by discontent; and tempted to repine, that the way to heaven lies through such humiliation and worldly disappointments; till the considerations, adduced in Faithful's answer, enable him at length to overcome this assailant, and to 'seek the honor that cometh from God only.'

Faithful: Yes, I met with Shame.—Persons of a peculiar turn of mind, when enabled to overcome temptations to discontent about worldly degradation, are exceedingly prone to be influenced by a false shame, and to profess religion in a timid and cautious manner; to be afraid of speaking all their mind in some places and companies, even when the most favorable opportunity occurs; to shun in part the society of those whom they most love and esteem, lest they should be involved in the contempt which is cast on them; to be reserved and inconstant in attending on the ordinances of God, entering a protest against vice and irreligion, bearing testimony to the truth, and in attempting to promote the Gospel: being apprehensive lest these things should deduct from their reputation for good sense, prudence, learning, or liberality of sentiment. Men who are least exposed to those conflicts in which Christian was engaged, are often most baffled by this enemy; nor can others make proper allowances for them in this case, any more than they can for such as experience those dark temptations, of which they have no conception. Constitution, habits, connections, extensive acquaintance with mankind, and an excess of sensibility, united to that pride which is common to man, continually suggest objections to every thing that the world despises, which they can hardly answer to themselves, and excite such alarms as they cannot get over; while a delicate sense of propriety, and the specious name of prudence, supply them with a kind of half-excuse for their timidity. The excessive trouble which this criminal and unreasonable shame occasions some persons, contrary to their judgment, convictions, arguments, endeavors, and prayers, gave our author the idea, that 'this enemy bears a wrong name.' Many a suggestion made to the mind, in this respect, from time to time, is so natural, and has so strong a party within (especially in those who are more desirous of honor than of wealth or pleasure,) that men can scarcely help feeling for the moment as if there were truth in it, though they know, upon reflection, that it is most irrational. Nay, these feelings insensibly warp men's conduct; though they are continually self-condemned on the retrospect. There are some who hardly ever get the better of this false shame; and it often brings their sincerity into doubt, both with themselves and others: but flourishing Christians at length in good measure rise superior to it, by such considerations as are here adduced, and by earnest persevering prayer.

Faithful: No, not I; for I had sunshine all the rest of the way through that, and also through the valley of the Shadow of Death.—Christian, in great measure, escaped the peculiar temptations that assaulted Faithful; yet he sympathized with him: nor did the latter deem the gloomy experiences of his brother visionary or imaginative, though he had been exempt from such trials. One man, from a complication of causes, is exposed to temptations of which another is ignorant; in this case he needs much sympathy, which he seldom meets with; while they, who are severe on him, are liable to be harassed and baffled in another way, which for want of coincidence in habit, temperature, and situation, he is equally prone to disregard. Thus believers are often led reciprocally to censure, suspect, despise, or dislike each other, on those very grounds which should render them useful and encouraging counsellors and companions.

CHAPTER XII

TALKATIVE

Faithful, as he chanced to look on one side, saw a man whose name was Talkative, walking at a distance beside them.—The character next introduced, under a most expressive name, is an admirable portrait, drawn by a masterly hand from some striking original, but exactly resembling numbers in every age and place, where the truths of the Gospel are generally known. Talkative is not thus called merely on account of his loquacity, but from the peculiarity of his religious profession, which gave scope to his natural propensity, by furnishing him with a copious subject, and enabling him to display his talents, or seek credit in the church, without the trouble and expense of experimental and practical godliness. Such vain talkers especially appear when religious profession is safe, cheap, and reputable; numbers keeping one another in countenance, preventing the odium of singularity, and even giving a prospect of secular advantage by connection with religious societies. They may, therefore, be expected in our age and nation, particularly in populous places, where the preaching or profession of any doctrine excites little attention or surprise, but ensures regard and favor from a numerous body who hold the same opinions. Such men appear above others, pushing themselves into notice, and becoming more conspicuous than humble believers; but their profession, specious at a distance, will not endure a near and strict investigation.

Faithful: But, by your leave, heavenly knowledge of these is the gift of God.—Zealous and lively Christians, who are not well established in judgment and experience, are often greatly taken with the discourse of persons who speak with great fluency and speciousness on various subjects, with a semblance of truth and piety; yet they sometimes feel, as it were, a defect in their harangues, which makes them hesitate, though they are easily satisfied with plausible explanations. Talkative's discourse is copied with surprising exactness from that of numbers, who learn doctrinally to discuss experimental subjects, of which they never felt the energy and efficacy in their own souls. Men of this stamp can take up any point in religion with great ease, and speak on it in a pompous ostentatious manner; but the humble believer forgets himself, while from his inmost heart he expatiates on topics which he longs to recommend to those whom he addresses. Humility and charity, however, dispose the possessors to make the best of others, and to distrust themselves: so that, unless these graces be connected with proportionable depth of judgment, and acuteness of discernment, they render them open to deception, and liable to be deceived by vain-glorious talkers. It would be conceited and uncandid, they think, to suspect a man, who says so many good things, with great confidence and zeal; their dissatisfaction with the conversation or sermon they suppose was their own fault; if they disagreed with the speaker, probably they were in error; if a doubt arose in their minds about his spirit or motives, it might be imputed to their own pride and envy. Thus men are seduced to sanction what they ought to protest against, and to admire those whom they should avoid; and that even by means of their most amiable dispositions. What follows is peculiarly calculated to rectify such mistakes, and to expose the consequences of this ill judged candor.

At this Christian modestly smiled, and said, This man, with whom you are so taken, will beguile with this tongue of his, twenty of them that know him not.—Those believers, who have made the most extensive and accurate observations on the state of religious profession in their own age and place, and are most acquainted with the internal history of the church in other lands, or former periods, may be deemed inferior in charity to their brethren; because they surpass them in penetration, and clearly perceive the mischiefs which arise from countenancing loose professors. They would vie with them in 'doing good to all men,' 'bearing with the infirmities of the weak,' 'restoring such men as are overtaken in a fault,' or in making allowances for the tempted; but they dare not sanction such professors as talk about religion and disgrace it, as mislead the simple, stumble the hopeful, prejudice the observing, and give enemies a plausible objection to the truth. Here charity constrains us to run the risk of being deemed uncharitable, by unmasking the hypocrite, and undeceiving the deluded. We must not indeed speak needlessly against any one, nor testify more than we know to be true, even against a suspected professor; but we should show, that vain talkers belong to the world, though numbers class them among religious people, to the great discredit of the cause.

Faithful: Well, I see that saying and doing are two things, and hereafter I shall better observe this distinction.—Talkative seems to have been introduced on purpose that the author might have a fair opportunity of stating his sentiments concerning the practical nature of religion, to which numbers in his day were too inattentive. This admired allegory has fully established the important distinction, between a dead and a living faith, on which the whole matter depends. We may boldly state every doctrine of grace, with all possible strength, and clearness, and every objection must ultimately fall to the ground, all abuses be excluded, provided this distinction be fully and constantly insisted on: for they arise without exception from substituting some false notion of faith in the place of that living, active, and efficacious principle, which the Scriptures so constantly represent as the grand peculiarity of vital godliness. The language used in this passage is precisely the same as is now branded with the opprobrious epithet of *legal*, by numbers who would be thought to admire the Pilgrim; as any impartial person must perceive, upon an attentive perusal of it: and, indeed, some expressions are used which they, who are accustomed to stand their trial before such as 'make a man an offender for a word,' have learned to avoid. 'The practice part' is accurately defined to be the unfailing effect of that inward life which is the soul of religion. True faith justifies indeed, as it forms the sinner's relation to, and union with Christ; but it always 'works by love,' and influences to obedience: hence the inquiry at the day of judgment will be rather about the inseparable fruits of faith, than its essential properties and nature.

Faithful: Well, I was not so fond of his company at

first, as I am sick of it now. What shall we do to be rid of him?—When we speak to loose professors, we should always keep two things in view; either to get rid of such ensnaring and dishonorable companions, or to use proper means to convince them of their fatal mistake. There is indeed more hope of the most ignorant and careless sinners than of them: yet 'with God all things are possible,' and we should not despair of any, especially as the very same method is suited to both the ends proposed; which the subsequent discourse most clearly evinces. Very plain and particular declarations of those things, by which true believers are distinguished from the most specious hypocrites (whether in conversation or preaching) are best calculated to undeceive and alarm false professors; and form the most commodious fan, by which the irreclaimable may be winnowed from the society of godly persons. This is of great importance; for they are Achans in the camp of Israel, spots and blemishes to every company that countenances them. Doctrinal or even practical discussions, if confined to general terms, will not startle them; they will mimic the language of experience, declaim against the wickedness of the world and the blindness of pharisees, and strenuously oppose the opinions held by some rival sect or party; they will endure the most awful declarations of the wrath of God against the wicked, supposing themselves to be unconcerned in them; nay, they will admit that they are backsliders, or inconsistent believers. But when the conversation or sermon compels them to complain, 'in so saying thou condemnest us also,' they will bear no longer, but seek refuge under more comfortable preachers, or in more candid company; and represent their faithful monitors as censorious, peevish, and melancholy men.

There is, therefore, knowledge and knowledge: knowledge that resteth in the bare speculation of things, and knowledge that is accompanied with the grace of faith and love.—Spiritual knowledge, obtained by an implicit belief of God's sure testimony under the teaching of the Holy Spirit, producing a hearty love of revealed truth, is always humbling, sanctifying, and transforming: but speculative knowledge is a mere notion of divine things, as distant from a man's own concern in them, or any due apprehension of their excellency and importance, which puffs up the heart with proud self-preference, feeds carnal and malignant passions, and leaves the possessor under the power of sin and Satan.

It gives him conviction of sin, especially of the defile-
ment of his nature, the sin of unbelief.—Divine teaching
convinces a man that he is justly condemned for his transgressions of the law, and cannot be saved unless he obtains an
interest in the merits of Christ by faith; and that unbelief, or
neglect of this great salvation, springs from pride, aversion to
the character, authority, and law of God, and love to sin and
the world; that it implies the guilt of treating the truth of God
as a lie, despising his wisdom and mercy, demanding happiness as a debt from his justice, and defying his 'wrath revealed
from heaven against all ungodliness and unrighteousness of
men.' This conviction makes way for his discovering the suit-
ableness to his case of a free salvation by faith: he perceives
the glory of the Divine perfections harmoniously displayed in
the person and redemption of Christ; and his heart is inwardly
drawn to close with the invitations of the Gospel, and to desire
above all things the fulfilment of its exceedingly great and precious promises to his soul. The expression 'revealed in him,'
is taken from St. Paul's account of his conversion (Galatians
1:16); but as that was extraordinary, without the intervention
of means or instruments, perhaps it is not accurately applied to
the ordinary experience of believers. Our author, however, evidently meant no more, than the illumination of the Holy Spirit
enabling a man to understand, believe, admire, and love the
truths of the Bible respecting Christ; and not any new revelation, declaring his interest in the Savior, by a whisper, vision,
or any such thing. These enthusiastic expectations and experiences have deceived many and stumbled more; and have done
greater harm to the cause of evangelical religion than can be
conceived or expressed.

The proverb is true of you which is said of a harlot,
to wit, that "She is a shame to all women;" so are you a
shame to all professors.—It is not enough to state practical
and experimental subjects in the plainest and most distinguishing manner: we ought also to apply them to men's consciences,
by the most solemn and particular interrogations. In public,
indeed, care must be taken, not to turn the thoughts of a congregation to an individual: yet we should aim to lead every one
to reflect on his own case, and excite his conscience to perform
the office of a faithful monitor. But in private, when we have
ground to suspect that men deceive themselves, such plain

dealing is the best evidence of disinterested love. It is at present, alas! much disused, and deemed inconsistent with politeness; so that, in many cases, an attempt of this kind would be considered as a direct outrage and insult: and perhaps in some circles, the language of these plain Pilgrims might be exchanged for that which would be less offensive, without deducting from its energy; yet zeal for the honor of the gospel, and love to the souls of men, are, no doubt, grievously sacrificed to urbanity in this age of courteous insincerity.

For he continuing (as I suppose he will do) as he is, would have been but a blot in our company: besides, the apostle says, "From such withdraw thyself."—This apostolic rule is of the greatest importance. While conscientious Christians, from a mistaken candor, tolerate scandalous professors, and associate with them, they seem to allow that they belong to the same family; and the world will charge their immoralities on the doctrines of the gospel, saying of those who profess them, 'They are all alike, if we could find them out.' But did all who 'adorn the doctrine of God our Savior,' withdraw from such men; their crimes would rest with themselves, and the world would be compelled to see the difference between hypocrites and real Christians. This is also the most effectual method of exciting self-deceivers or inconsistent professors to self-examination, and of thus bringing them to be *ashamed* and humbled in true repentance: and, at the same time, it tends to deprive such men of that influence, which they often employ to mislead and pervert hopeful inquirers and unestablished believers. Even the best conducted discipline would have but a partial effect in preventing these evils, if not followed up by this conduct of individuals; and, where the former cannot be obtained, the latter would produce happier consequences than believers in general would suppose.

CHAPTER XIII

VANITY FAIR

Set your faces like a flint; you have all power in heaven and earth on your side.—The author, intending in the next place to represent his Pilgrims as exposed to severe persecution, and to exhibit in one view what Christians should expect, and may be exposed to, from the enmity of the world, very judiciously introduces that interesting scene by Evangelist's meeting them, with suitable cautions, exhortations, and encouragements. The minister, by whose faithful labors a man is first directed into the way of salvation, commonly retains great influence, and is considered with special affection, even when various circumstances have placed him at a distance under some other pastor. The conversation therefore, of such a beloved friend tends to recall to the minds of believers their former fears, trials, and deliverances, which animates them to encounter further difficulties, and opens the way for seasonable counsels and admonitions.

Quit yourselves like men; and commit the keeping of your souls to your God in well-doing, as unto a faithful Creator.—The able and faithful minister can foretell many things, from his knowledge of the Scriptures, and enlarged experience and observation, of which his people are not aware. He knows beforehand, that 'through much tribulation they must enter into the kingdom of God;' and the circumstances of the times aid him in discerning what trials and difficulties more especially await them. A retired life shelters a believer from the enmity of the world: and timid men are often tempted on this account to abide *in the wilderness;* to choose obscurity and solitude for the sake of quiet and safety, to the neglect of those active services for which they are qualified. But when Christians are called forth to more public situations, they need peculiar cautions and instructions: for inexperience renders men inattentive to the words of Scripture; and they often do not at all expect, or prepare for, the trials which are inseparable from those scenes, on which they are perhaps even impatient to enter.

The ware of Rome and her merchandise is greatly promoted in this fair: only our English nation, with some others, have taken a dislike thereat.—Our author evidently designed to exhibit in his allegory the grand outlines of the difficulties, temptations, and sufferings, to which believers are exposed in this evil world; which, in a work of this nature, must be related as if they came upon them one after another in regular succession; though in actual experience several may meet together, many may molest the same person again and again, and some harass him in every stage of his journey. We should, therefore, singly consider the instruction conveyed by every allegorical incident, without measuring our experience, or calculating our progress, by comparing them with *circumstances*, which might be reversed or altered with almost endless variety. In general, Vanity Fair represents the wretched state of things, in those populous places especially where true religion is neglected and persecuted, and indeed of 'the whole world lying in wickedness,' as distinguished from the church of redeemed sinners. This continues the same (in respect of the general principles, conduct, and pursuits of mankind), through all ages and nations: but Christians are called to mix more with it at some times than at others; and Satan, the god and prince of it, is permitted to excite fierce persecution in some places, and on some occasions, while at other times he is restrained. Many, therefore, seem to spend all their days in the midst of Vanity Fair, and of continual insults or injuries; while others are only sometimes thus exposed, and pass most of their lives unmolested: and a few are favored with so obscure a situation, and such peaceable times, that they are very little acquainted with these trials. Mr. Bunyan, living in the country, had frequent opportunities of witnessing those Fairs, which are held first in one town and then in another; and of observing the pernicious effects produced on the principles, morals, health, and circumstances of young persons especially, by thus drawing together a multitude, from motives of interest, dissipation and excess. He must also, doubtless, have found them to be a very dangerous snare to serious or hopeful persons: so that his delineation of this case under allusions taken from this scene, will be more interesting and affecting to those who have been spectators of it, than to such as have moved in higher circles, or dwelt chiefly in populous cities. Worldly men covet, pursue, grasp at, and contend for the things of time and sense, with eagerness and violence, so that their whole conduct aptly resembles the bustle, selfishness, artifice, dissipation, riot, and tumult of a large crowded Fair. The profits, pleasures, honors, possessions, and distinctions of the world, are as transient and frivolous as the events of the fair-day; with which the children are delighted, but which every man of sense contemns. Solomon, after a complete experiment, pronounced the whole to be 'vanity of vanities:' the veriest vanity imaginable, a complex vanity, an accumulation of ciphers, a lottery consisting entirely of blanks; every earthly object being unsuitable to the wants of the rational soul, unsubstantial, unsatisfactory, and perishing. Yet this traffic of vanities is kept up *all the year:* because the carnal mind always hankers after one worldly trifle or other, and longs 'for change of follies and relays of joy;' while objects suited to its feverish thirst are always at hand to allure it, deriving their efficacy from continually pressing, as it were, on the senses. When our first parents were fatally prevailed on to join Satan's apostasy, they 'forsook the fountain of living waters, to hew out to themselves broken cisterns;' and the idolatry of seeking happiness from the creature instead of the Creator, has been universal among all their posterity. Since the promise of a Savior opened to fallen men a door of hope, the tempter has continually tried to allure them by outward objects, or induce them by the dread of pain and suffering to 'neglect so great salvation.' Thus the prince of the devils sets up this *Fair;* and by teaching men to abuse the good creatures of God to vile purposes, or to expect from them such satisfaction as they were never meant to afford, he has used them as baits to the ambition, avarice, levity, and sensuality of the carnal mind. No crime has ever been committed on earth, or conceived in the heart of man, which did not arise from this universal apostasy and idolatry; from the excess, to which the insufficiency of the object to answer the proposed end, gives rise; and from the vile passions which the jarring interests or inclinations of number-less competitors for honor, power, wealth, and pleasure, cannot fail to excite. As the streams of impiety and vice, which flow from this source, are varied, according to men's constitutions, educations, habits and situations; so different worldly pursuits predominate in divers nations, or stages of civilization. Hence the manifold variations in the human character, which equal the diversity of their complexions, shape or capacities, though they be all of one nature. To this an allusion is made by 'the rows' in this Fair. The merchandise of Rome, which suited a rude and ignorant age, has now given place to the more plausi-ble wares of sceptical philosophers which are more agreeable to the pride of learning and human reasoning. Even things lawful in themselves, when sought, or possessed in a manner which is not consistent with "seeking *first* the kingdom of God, and his righteousness," become allurements of Satan to draw sinners into his fatal snare.

This fair, therefore, is an ancient thing, of long stand-ing, and a very great fair.—Christianity does not allow men to 'bury their talent in the earth,' or to put 'their light under a bushel:' they should not 'go out of the world,' or retire into clois-ters and deserts: and therefore, they must all go through this Fair. Thus our Lord and Savior endured all the temptations and sufferings of this evil world, without being at all impeded or entangled by them, or stepping in the least aside to avoid them. The age in which he lived peculiarly abounded in all possible allurements; and he was exposed to such enmity, con-tempt, and sufferings, as could never be exceeded or equalled. But 'he went about doing good;' and his whole conduct, as well as his indignant repulse of the tempter's insolent offer, hath emphatically shown his judgment of all earthly things, and exhibited to us 'an example that we should follow his steps.'

Here are inserted the following lines:—

> 'Behold Vanity Fair! The Pilgrims there
> Are chained, and stoned beside:
> Even so it was our Lord past here,
> And on Mount Calvary died.'

"Turn away mine eyes from beholding vanity;" and look upwards, signifying that their trade and traffic was in heaven.—The presence of real Christians in those places, where a large concourse of worldly men are collected for sinful purposes, must produce a disturbance and effervescence; and the smaller the number is of those who by their actions, words, or silence, protest against vice and impiety, the fiercer the opposition that will be excited. A pious clergyman on board a vessel, where he was a single exception to the general ungodliness that prevailed, gave offence by constantly but silently withdrawing, when oaths or unseemly discourse made his situation uneasy; and he was called to account for so assuming a singularity! Consistent believers, appearing in character among worldly people, and not disguising their sentiments, always excite this opposition: but more accommodating professors escape it. An avowed dependence on the righteousness and atonement of Christ for acceptance, gives vast offence to those who rely on their own good works for justification: and conformity to the example, and obedience to the commandments of the Redeemer, are deemed precise and uncouth in the judgment of those who 'walk according to the course of this world;' and they deem the Christian *insane* or *outlandish* for his peculiarities. His discourse, seasoned with piety, humility, and spirituality, so differs from the 'filthy conversation of the wicked,' and the polite dissimulation of the courtly, that they can have no intercourse with him, or he with them: and when *he* speaks of the love of Christ, and the satisfaction of communion with Him, while *they* 'blaspheme the worthy name by which he is called;' they must seem *barbarians* each to the other. But above all, the believer's contempt of worldly things, when they interfere with the will and glory of God, forms such a testimony against all the pursuits and conduct of carnal men, as must excite their greatest astonishment and indignation; while he shuns with dread and abhorrence, as incompatible with salvation, those very things to which they wholly addict themselves without the least remorse.

They took them, and beat them, and besmeared them with dirt, and then put them into the cage, that they might be made a spectacle to all the men of the fair.— When the scoffs of those, 'who think it strange that Christians will not run with them to the same excess of riot,' extort from them a full and explicit declaration of their principles, it may be expected that the reproaches and insults of their despisers will be increased; and then all the mischief and confusion which follow will be laid to their charge—'There were no such disputes about religion before they came;' 'These men who turn the world upside down are come hither also;' 'they exceedingly trouble the city,' town or village by their uncharitable discourse and example! Thus Satan takes occasion to excite persecution, when he fears lest the servants of God should successfully disseminate their principles: and persecuting princes and magistrates, his 'most trusty friends,' are deputed by him to molest and punish their *peaceable* subjects, for conscientiously refusing conformity to the world, or for dissenting from doctrines and modes of worship which they deem unscriptural. Thus the most valuable members of the community are banished, imprisoned, or murdered; multitudes are tempted to hypocrisy: encouragement is given to timeservers to seek secular advantages by acting contrary to their consciences; the principles of sincerity and integrity are generally weakened or destroyed by multiplied prevarications and false professions; and numerous instruments of cruelty and oppression are involved in this complication of atrocious crimes. Our author doubtless drew many of his portraits, in the subsequent historical picture, from originals then sufficiently known; and if any think that he has heightened his colorings, it may furnish them with a subject for gratitude, and a reason for content and peaceable submission to our rulers. In Fox's Martyrs we meet with authenticated facts, that fully equal this allegorical representation: nay, 'The Acts of the Apostles' give us the very same view of the subject.

Wherefore they threatened, that neither cage nor irons should serve their turn, but that they should die for the abuse they had done, and for deluding the men of the fair.—The contempt, injustice, and cruelty, with which persecutors treat the harmless disciples of Christ, gives them an occasion of discovering that amiable conduct and spirit which accord to the precepts of Scripture, and the example of persecuted prophets and apostles; and this often produces the most happy effects on those who are less prejudiced, which still more exasperates determined opposers; yet it frequently procures a short respite for the persecuted, while worldly people quarrel about them among themselves. And even if greater severity be at length determined on, persevering prudence, meekness, and patience, amidst all the rage of their enemies, will bear testimony for them in the consciences of numbers; their religion will appear beautiful, in proportion as their persecutors expose their own odious deformity. God will be with them to comfort and deliver them; he will be honored by their profession and behavior, and many will derive the most important advantage, from their patient sufferings and cheerful fortitude in adhering to the truths of the gospel. But when believers are put off their guard by ill usage; when their zeal is rash, contentious, boasting, or disproportionate; when they are provoked to render 'railing for railing,' or to act contrary to the plain precepts of Scripture: they bring guilt on their consciences, stumble their brethren, harden the hearts, and open the mouths of opposers, dishonor God and the gospel, and gratify the great enemy of souls; who malignantly rejoices in their misconduct, but is tortured when they endure sufferings in a proper manner.

And as to the king you talk of, since he is Beelzebub, the enemy of our Lord, I defy him and all his angels.— The description of the process, instituted against the Pilgrims, is given in language taken from the legal forms used in our courts of justice, which in Mr. Bunyan's days were shamefully perverted to subserve the most iniquitous oppressions. The allegorical narrative is framed in such a manner, as emphatically to expose the *secret* reasons, which influence men to persecute their inoffensive neighbors; and the very names employed declare the several corrupt principles of the heart, from whence this atrocious conduct results. Enmity against God, and his holy character, law, worship, truth, and servants, is the principal source of persecution—the judge in Faithful's trial. The interference of spiritual religion with men's covetous ambitious, and sensual pursuits; and the interruption it gives to their false peace, and unanimity in ungodliness or hypocrisy, which it tends to expose and undermine, form the grounds of the indictment: that is, when the persecuted can truly answer, that they 'only set themselves against that which sets itself against Him, who is higher than the highest;' and when they do not suffer 'as evil doers, busy bodies in other men's matters,' ambitious competitors for secular advantages, or contentious disputants about political questions.

They were then asked, if they knew the prisoner at the bar, and what they had to say for their lord the king against him.—The names of these witnesses declare the character of the most active instruments of persecution. Even Pilate could perceive that the Jewish Scribes and Priests were actuated by *envy*, in delivering up Jesus to him. His instructions discredited theirs, and diminished their reputation and influence; he was more followed than they: and in proportion as he was deemed a teacher sent from God, they were disregarded as blind guides. Thus formal instructors, and learned men, who are strangers to the power of godliness, have always affected to despise the professors and preachers of the gospel as ignorant enthusiasts. They envy the reputation acquired by them, and are angry at the success of their doctrines. If they have not the authority to silence the *ministers*, they will browbeat such of his hearers as are within the reach of their influence; especially if they have affronted them by forsaking their uninteresting instructions. If they cannot prevail upon 'the powers that be' to interfere; they will employ reproaches, menaces, or even oppression, to obstruct the progress of evangelical ministers; should any obsolete law remain unrepealed, of which they can take advantage, they will be the first to enforce it; and if the rulers engage in persecution, they will take the lead as prosecutors and witnesses. As this was remarkably the case in our author's days; and as the history of the old and new Testament, and every authentic-record of persecutions, give the same view of it; we cannot be greatly at a loss to know what was especially meant by this emblem. In other respects there is seldom much in the circumstances of pious persons, to excite the *envy* of their ungodly neighbors; as they despise their spiritual privileges and comforts.

He neither regardeth prince nor people, law nor custom, but doth all that he can to possess all men with certain of his disloyal notions, which he in the general calls "principles of faith and holiness."—It has always been the practice of envious accusers to represent those, who refuse religious conformity, as *disloyal* and disaffected to the civil government of their country; because they judge it 'right to obey God rather than man!' How grievous then is it, that any, who profess the gospel, should give plausibility to such calumnies! How desirable for them, after the example, and in obedience to the precepts of Christ and his Apostles, 'by well doing to put to silence the ignorance of foolish men,' 'to avoid all appearance of evil,' 'to render to Caesar the things that are Caesar's,' and to constrain even enemies to bear testimony to their peaceable

deportment! This would exhibit their patient suffering for conscience' sake as amiable and respectable, in the eyes of all not
immediately engaged in persecution; and would give a sanction
to their most bold and decided testimony against every kind of
vice, impiety, and false religion. But when they revile the persons of rulers, or make religion the pretext for intermeddling
out of their place in political matters, and in attempting to disturb the peace of the community; they exceedingly strengthen
men's prejudices against the doctrines of the gospel, and the
whole body of those who profess them; and thus give occasion,
and furnish an excuse, for that very persecution of which they
complain, in other respects with the greatest justice.

*That we still do worship in vain, are yet in our sins,
and finally shall be damned: and this is that which I
have to say.*—Superstition represents another class of under-
ling persecutors; (for the principals are often masked infidels.)
Traditions, human inventions, forms and externals, appear
to them decent, venerable and sacred; and are mistaken with
pertinacious ignorance, for the substance of religion. As mere
circumstances of worship, some of these may very well answer
the purpose; provided they be not *imposed,* magnified above
their value, or substituted in the place of things essentially
good: others are bad, in their origin, use and tendency; yet the
truths, ordinances and commandments of God are made void
that men may keep them! What is pompous or burdensome
appears to such men meritorious; and the excitement of mere
natural passions, (as at a tragedy,) is deemed a most needful
help to true devotion. They are, therefore, eminently qualified
to be witnesses against the faithful servants of God: for they
'think they are thus doing him service,' while they are opposing a company of profane despisers of their idolized forms; a set
of fanatics, heretics, and pestilent schismatics! Their religious
zeal contracts and hardens their hearts; and the supposed
goodness of the cause sanctifies their bitter rage, enmity and
calumny. The extreme odiousness of these proceedings should
excite all who love the truth, to keep at the utmost distance
from such obstinate confidence and violence; to discountenance
them to the utmost, in the zealots of their own sentiments;
and to leave the enemies of the gospel, if possible, to monopo-
lize this disgrace. For, hitherto, almost all parties have been
betrayed into it, when advanced to power; and this has given

the enemies of Christianity their most plausible arguments against it.

Calling you an ungodly villain, with many other such-like vilifying terms, with which he hath bespattered most of the gentry of our town.—Pickthank represents a set of tools that persecutors continually use; namely, men of no religious principle; who assume the appearance of zeal for any party, as may best promote their interests; and who inwardly despise both the superstitious and the spiritual worshipper. These men discern little in the conduct or circumstances of believers to excite either their rage, or envy; but if their superiors be disposed to persecute, they will afford their assistance; for preferment runs in this channel. So that they bear their testimony from avarice or ambition, and flatter the most execrable characters, in order to get forward in the world: this being the grand object to which they readily sacrifice every thing else. The names of those against whom Faithful spoke, show that his *crime* consisted in protesting, by word and deed, against vices, which the great too often think themselves privileged to commit without censure; and not in reviling the persons, or misrepresenting the actions of superiors. The former may with great propriety be done at all times; and on some occasions the testimony against sin cannot be too closely applied to the consciences of the guilty, without respect of persons; but the latter is always unjust and unscriptural.

The prince of this town, with all the rabblement, his attendants, by this gentleman named, are more fit for being in hell than in this town and country; and so the Lord have mercy upon me.—Faithful's defense is introduced by these lines, as in the foregoing instances:—

> 'Now, Faithful, play the man, speak for thy God;
> Fear not the wicked's malice, nor their rod:
> Speak boldly, man, the truth is on thy side;
> Die for it, and to life in triumph ride.'

Christians in such circumstances should be more concerned for the honor of God than for their own credit or safety; and they should take occasion to bear a decided testimony to the truths, commandments and institutions of the Scripture: leaving it to their accusers, judges, or hearers, to determine what sentiments or practices are thus proved to be anti-christian, or what numbers of 'teachers in Israel' are exposed as blind guides. That faith, (by which alone we approach to God, and acceptably worship him,) has no other object than divine revelation; nothing done without the *express warrant* of Scripture can be profitable to eternal life, whatever may be said for its expediency; but every thing foisted into religion contrary to that sacred rule must be an abomination. Human faith may please men; but without a divine faith it is impossible to please God, either in general or any particular action. And, as we can seldom speak against the vile lusts of men, without being judged by implication to rail against such as are notoriously addicted to them, we cannot be the followers of Him, 'whom the world hated, because he testified of it that its works were evil,' unless we be willing to risk all consequences in copying his example.

You see he disputeth against our religion; and for the treason that he hath already confessed he deserveth to die the death.—A more just and keen satirical description of such *legal* iniquities, can scarcely be imagined, than that contained in this passage. The statutes and precedents adduced, (with a humorous and well imitated reference to the style and manner, in which charges are commonly given to juries;) show what patterns persecuting legislators and magistrates choose to copy, and whose kingdom they labor to uphold. Nor can any impartial man deny, that the inference is fair which our author meant the reader to deduce; namely, that *nominal* protestants, enacting laws requiring conformity to their own creeds and forms, and inflicting punishments on such as peaceably dissent from them, are actually involved in the guilt of these heathen persecutors, and of their anti-christian successors; even if their doctrine and worship be allowed to be scriptural and spiritual. For these methods only serve to promote hypocrisy, and to expose the conscientious to the malice, envy or avarice of the unprincipled.

Thus came Faithful to his end.—The names of the jurymen and their general and particular verdicts, the cruel execution of Faithful, and the happy event of his sufferings, need no comment. It was not indeed the practice of the times in which our author lived, to inflict death on those who were persecuted for conscience' sake: yet very great rigors were used; the system then adopted, if carried to its consequences, must have ended in the extermination of all nonconformists from the land; it was natural to expect still greater cruelty from persons who were found capable of the severities already experienced; and without all doubt many actually lost their lives, in one way or other, by the persecutions to which they were exposed. All those, who feel a disposition to employ the power of the magistrate against such as differ from them in religious matters, should attentively consider the contemptible and odious picture here delineated with the most entire justice, of the whole race of persecutors, and of their characters, principles, motives, and conduct: that they may learn to hate and dread such an anti-christian practice, and shun the most remote approaches to it. On the other hand, they who are exposed to persecution, or in danger of it, should study the character and conduct of Faithful, that they may learn to suffer in a Christian spirit, and to adorn the gospel in the fiery trial. The following lines are here introduced as before:

> 'Brave Faithful! bravely done in word and deed!
> Judge, witnesses, and jury have, instead
> Of overcoming thee, but shown their rage,
> When they are dead, thou'lt live from age to age.'

But He that overrules all things, having the power of their rage in his own hand, so wrought it about, that Christian for that time escaped them, and went his way.—When the believer has done his work, the wrath of man may be permitted to expedite his removal to his heavenly inheritance; but all the malice and power of earth and hell are utterly unavailing to cut off any one till the purposes of God respecting him are accomplished. Thus the Apostles were preserved during Saul's persecution, and Peter was rescued from the hands of Herod. The Lord has various methods of protecting and liberating his servants: sometimes he intimidates their persecutors; the paroxysm of their fury abates; or they are disheartened by ill success in their efforts to extirpate the hated sect; the principles and instruments are left to quarrel among themselves; their cruelties disgust the people, so that they dare not proceed: political interests engage even ungodly princes to promote toleration, and chain up the demon persecution: or the Lord raises up one of his own servants to authority, that he may be a protector of his church, and disappoint the devices of his enemies.

CHAPTER XIV

CHRISTIAN AND HOPEFUL

This Hopeful also told Christian, that there were many more of the men in the fair that would take their time, and follow after.—'The blood of the martyrs is the seed of the church:' for sufferings, properly endured, form the most convincing and useful kind of preaching. The name of Christian's new companion denotes the opinion, which established believers form at first, of such as begin to profess the gospel in an intelligent manner. The nature of an allegory rendered it impracticable to introduce the new convert, as beginning his pilgrimage from the same place, or going through the same scenes, as Christian had done: neither could Faithful, for the same reason, be represented as passing the *river* afterward mentioned. But the *brotherly covenant*, in which Hopeful joined himself with his companion, must be supposed to imply the substance of all that had been spoken of, as necessary to final acceptance.

When Religion goes in his silver slippers; we love much to walk with him in the streets, if the sun shines, and the people applaud him.—The character of By-ends, and the group that attended him, forms a clear detection and merited condemnation of a large company of false professors; and is not at all inferior in importance to the preceding severe satire on open persecutors. When rest is given to the church, hypocrites often multiply more than real Christians. The name of this man, and those of his town and relations, do not merely describe his original character and situation, (as Christian was at first called Graceless of the City of Destruction;) but they denote the nature of his religious profession. Believers look back on their former principles and behavior with shame and abhorrence; but hypocrites, when reproved for evident sins, excuse them, because Christ came to save the lost, and because he is merciful to the chief of sinners. Christian would readily have granted that 'no good lived' at his native city; and on that very account he had renounced it with all his old connections; but By-ends hoped better of Fair-speech, and gloried in his honorable relations there. Yet he was ashamed of his *name;* for men are unwilling to allow that they seek nothing more than worldly advantages by religion. The names here selected are most emphatically descriptive of that whole company of professed Christians, who, under various pretences, suppose that 'gain is godliness.' The polite *simulation* and *dissimulation*, which some most courtly writers have inculcated, as the summit of good breeding, the perfection of a finished education, and the grand requisite for obtaining consequence in society if introduced into religion, and adopted by professors or preachers of the gospel, in connection with fashionable accomplishments and an agreeable address, constitute the most versatile, refined, and insinuating species of *hypocrisy* that can be imagined: and a man of talents, of any occupation or profession, may render it very subservient to his interest; by insuring the patronage or custom of those to whom he attaches himself, without giving much umbrage to the world, which may indeed despise such a character, but will not deem him worthy of hatred. He may assume any of the names here provided for him, as may best suit his line in life; and may shape his course, in subserviency to his grand concern, with considerable latitude; provided he has prudence enough to keep clear of scandalous vices: he will not be long in learning the beneficial art of using two tongues with one mouth, and of looking one way and rowing another, and perhaps he may improve his fortune by an honorable alliance, with some branch of the ancient family of the Feignings. The grand difference betwixt this whole tribe, and the body of true Christians, consists in these two things: Christians seek the salvation of their souls, and at the same time aim to glorify God, and be useful to their neighbors; but hypocrites profess to be religious in order to obtain friends, patrons, customers, or applause: those follow the Lord habitually, whatever tribulations arise because of the word; but these conceal or deny their profession, when, instead of gaining by it, they are exposed to reproach or persecution.

If I take not my mark amiss, I deem I have half a guess of you: is not your name Mr. By-ends, of Fair-speech?— The people of the world, who avow their real character, know how to serve Mammon by neglecting and despising God and religion; and the disciples of Christ can serve God by renouncing the world and its friendship: but time-servers talk as if they had found but the secret of uniting these two discordant interests, and thus of 'knowing something more than all the world.' This is the most prominent feature in this group of portraits, which in other respects exhibits great dissimilarities, and contains the faces of persons belonging to every division of professed Christians on earth.

I must do as I did before you overtook me, even go by myself, until some overtake me that will be glad of my company.—When hypocrites are charged with their double-dealing and obvious crimes, they commonly set it down to the account of persecution, and class themselves with that blessed company, of whom 'all manner of evil is spoken *falsely*, for the name of Christ:' as if there were no difference between suffering as a Christian, and being a scandal to the very name of Christianity! Thus they endeavor to quiet their minds, and keep up their credit; deeming themselves at the same time very *prudent* and *fortunate*, in shifting about so as to avoid the cross, and secure their temporal interests. The Apostle says concerning these men, 'from such turn away,' and the decided manner in which Christian warns By-ends, and renounces his company, though perhaps too plain to be either approved or imitated in this courtly candid age, is certainly warranted and required by the Holy Scriptures.

Money-love: Alas! why did they not stay, that we might have had their good company? for they, and we, and you, sir, I hope, are all going on pilgrimage.—It might have been supposed that the persons, here introduced, were settled inhabitants of the Town of Vanity, or the City of Destruction: but indeed they professed themselves Pilgrims, and desired during the sunshine to associate with Pilgrims; provided they would allow them, to *hold the world, love money*, and *save all*, whatever became of faith and holiness, of honesty, piety, truth, and charity! Covetousness, whether it consist in rapaciously trying to get money, to hoard or to lavish, in purchasing consequence, power, or pleasure, or in supporting magnificence and the pride of life; or in parsimony as to the ordinary proportion of expenditure; or in tenacity, when duty requires a man to part with it; is a vice not so easily defined as many others. At the same time it enables a man, in various ways, to reward those who can be induced to connive at it, and to render it dangerous to oppose him: so that it is not wonderful that it generally finds more quarter, even among religious persons, than other vices, which are not marked with so black a brand in the Holy Scriptures. Too many, professing to be the disciples of Christ, 'bless the covetous, whom God abhorreth,' and speak to them as if they were doubtless true Christians; because of their steadiness in the profession of a doctrinal system, and a mode of worship; attended by morality, where money is not concerned and scandal might be incurred; and a narrow disproportionate contribution from their abundance, to support the interest of a society or a party. Thus the 'vile person is called liberal, and the churl is said to be bountiful:' and the idolatry of worshipping money has seldom been execrated equally with that of them, 'whose god is their belly;' unless when so enormous as to become a kind of insanity. The most frugal support of religious worship, with the most disinterested pastors and managers, is attended with an expense that the poor of the flock are utterly unable to defray: by this opening, Hold-the-world and Money-love frequently obtain admission, and acquire undue influence among Pilgrims. And when the effect of remaining selfishness in the hearts of true believers, insinuating itself under the specious plea of prudence and necessity, and the ill consequences of specious hypocrites associating with them, are duly considered; with the censure that must fall upon a few obscure individuals who attempt to stem the torrent; it will appear evident that the rich, and they who are growing rich have more need of self-examination and jealousy over their own hearts than any other persons; because they will be less plainly warned and reproved, in public and private, than their inferiors.

Save-all: That's bad: but we read of some that are "righteous over-much;" and such men's rigidness prevails with them to judge and condemn all but themselves.— This expression of Solomon was probably intended to caution us against excessive zeal for some detached parts of religion to the neglect of others, or against superstitious austerities and enthusiastical delusions, or any extremes, which always lead men off from vital godliness: or, as some think, it is the objection of an opponent, which he afterward answers: but it is the constant plea of those, who neglect the most essential duties of their place and station, to avoid the cross, and preserve their worldly interests; and thus 'they wrest the Scriptures to their own destruction.'

But he must not be such as the men before us, if they be as you have described them.—This dialogue is not in the least more absurd and selfish, than the discourse of many who attend on the preaching of the gospel, and expect to be thought believers. They connect 'the wisdom of the serpent' with his craft and malice, not with the harmlessness of the dove: if worldly lucre be the honey, they imitate the bee, and only attend to religion when they can gain by it: they cut and shape their creed and conduct to suit the times, and to please those among whom they live: they determine to keep what they have at any rate, and to get more, if it can be done without open scandal; never seriously recollecting that they are mere stewards of providential advantages, of which a strict account must at last be given; and, instead of willingly renouncing or expending them, for the Lord's sake, when his providence or commandment requires it, they determine to hoard them up for themselves and families, or spend them in worldly indulgence; and then quote and pervert Scripture to varnish over this base idolatry.

Since he is improved in his parts and industry thereby, be counted as one that pursues his call, and the opportunity put into his hand to do good.—There is a fund of satirical humor in the supposed case here very gravely stated; and if the author, in his accurate observations on mankind, selected his example from among the mercenaries that are the scandal of the established church, her most faithful friends will not greatly resent this conduct of a dissenter. The *worthy* clergyman seeks *first* (not 'the kingdom of God and his righteousness,' or the glory of God in the salvation of souls, but) a rich benefice: to attain this primary object, means must be used; and *hypocritical* pretensions to diligence, zeal, piety, with some change of doctrine, merely to please men, seem most likely to succeed, and so this most base, prevaricating, selfish and ungodly plan is adopted! In how many thousand of instances has this been an awful reality? How often has it been pleaded for, as prudent and laudable, by men, not only pretending to common honesty and sincerity, but calling themselves the disciples of Jesus Christ!

And if they are mute when dealt with by vessels of clay, what will they do when they shall be rebuked by the flames of a devouring fire?—God permits Satan to bait his own hook with some worldly advantage, in order to induce men to renounce their profession, expose their hypocrisy, or disgrace the gospel: and they (poor deluded mortals!) call it 'an opening of Providence.' The Lord indeed puts the object in their way, if they will break his commandments in order to seize upon it: but he does this in order to prove them, and to show whether they most love him or their worldly interests; and it is the devil that tempts them to seize the advantage by sinful compliances or hypocritical pretences that he may 'take them captive at his will.' The arguments here adduced, by an admirable imitation of the pleas often used on such occasions, are only valid on the supposition that religion is a mere external appearance, and has nothing to do with the state of the heart and affections; and in short, that *hypocrisy* and *piety* are words precisely of the same meaning. Upon the whole, the answer of Christian, though somewhat rough, is so apposite and conclusive, that it is sufficient to fortify every honest and attentive mind against all the arguments, which the whole tribe of time-serving professors of Christianity ever did, or ever can adduce, in support of their ingenious schemes and assiduous efforts to reconcile religion with covetousness and love of the world, or to render them subservient to their secular interests.

The ground, being deceitful under them, broke, and they were slain: some also had been maimed there, and could not to their dying day be their own men again.—When the church enjoys outward peace and prosperity (which has been generally but for a transient season), they, who profess the gospel, are peculiarly exposed to the temptation of seeking worldly riches and distinctions which at other times were placed at such a distance as to lose most of their attractive influence; and many in such circumstances are more disconcerted and disposed to murmur, if excluded from sharing these idolized prizes, than Christians appear to have been under the most cruel persecutions. But the Hill LUCRE, with the silver mine, is *a little out* of the Pilgrim's path, even in times of the greatest outward rest and security: and while those 'who *will* be rich fall into temptation and a snare, and into many foolish and hateful lusts, which drown men in destruction and perdition:' others, forgetting that 'the love of money is the root of all evil, having coveted after it, have erred from the faith, and pierced themselves through with many sorrows.'

Over against the silver mine, stood Demas (gentle-man-like) to call passengers to come and see; who said to Christian and his fellow, Ho! turn aside hither, and I will show you a thing.—We know not in what way the love of this present world influenced Demas to forsake St. Paul: and it is not agreed whether he afterward repented, or whether he was finally an apostate: yet our author is warranted by the general opinion in thus using his name, and afterward joining it with those of Gehazi, Judas, and others, who perished by that idolatry. The love of money does not always spring from a desire of covetously hoarding it: but often from a vain affecta-tion of gentility which is emphatically implied by the epithet *gentleman-like*, bestowed on Demas. The connections that pro-fessors form in a day of ease and prosperity, and the example of the world around them, and even that of numbers who would be thought to love the gospel, seduce them insensibly into a style of living that they cannot afford, in order to avoid the imputation of being sordid and singular. An increasing family insures additional expenses, and children *genteelly* educated naturally expect to be provided for accordingly. Thus debts are contracted and gradually accumulate: it is neither so easy nor reputable to retrench, as it was to launch out: and numerous tempters induce men thus circumstanced to turn aside to the Hill Lucre; that is, to leave the direct path of probity and piety, that they may obtain supplies to their urgent and clamorous necessities. Young persons when they first set out in life, often lay the foundation for innumerable evils, by vainly emulat-ing the expensive style of those in the same line of business, or the same rank in the community, who are enabled to sup-port such expenses, either by extensive dealings or unjustifi-able means. Many are the bankruptcies, which originate from this mistaken conduct: and besides this, it is often found, that fair profits are inadequate to uphold the appearance which was at first needlessly assumed; so that *necessity* is pleaded for engaging in those branches of trade, or seizing on those emoluments, which the conduct of worldly people screens from total scandal, but which are evidently contrary to the word of God, and the plain rule of exact truth and rectitude; and which render their consciences very uneasy. But who can bear the mortification of owning himself poorer than he was thought to be? Who dare risk the consequences of being suspected to be insolvent? In these ensnaring circumstances, professed Christians, if not powerfully influenced by religious principles, will be almost sure to embrace Demas's invitation, along with By-ends, Money-love, and Save-all; and if they be 'not drowned in destruction and perdition,' will 'fall into temptation and a snare, and pierce themselves through with many sorrows.' It therefore is incumbent on every one, well to consider, that it is as *unjust* to contract debts for superfluous indulgences, or to obtain credit by false appearances of affluence, as it is to defraud by any other imposition: and that this kind of *dishonesty* makes way for innumerable temptations to more disgraceful species of the same crime: not to speak of its absolute inconsistency with piety and charity.

But none are in this respect so much exposed as ministers and their families, when, having no private fortune, they are situated among the affluent and genteel: and by yielding to this temptation, they are often incapacitated from paying their debts with punctuality: they are induced to degrade their office by stooping to unsuitable methods of extricating themselves out of difficulties, from which strict frugality would have preserved them, and by laying themselves under obligations to such men as are capable of abusing their purchased superiority; and, above all, they are generally led to place their children in situations and connections highly unfavorable to the interests of their souls, in order to procure them a genteel provision. If we form our judgment on this subject from the Holy Scriptures, we shall not think of finding the true ministers of Christ among the higher classes in the community, *in matters of external appearance or indulgence.* That information and learning which many of them have the opportunity of acquiring, may render them acceptable company to the affluent, especially to such as love them for their work's sake; and even the exercise of Christian tempers will improve the urbanity acquired by a liberal education, where faithfulness is not concerned. But if a minister thinks, that the attention of the great or noble requires him to copy their expensive style of living, he grievously mistakes the matter. For this will generally forfeit the opinion before entertained of his good sense and regard to propriety: and his *official* declarations, concerning the vanity of earthly things, and the Christian's indifference to them, will be suspected of insincerity; while it is observed, that he conforms to the world, as far or even further than his circumstances will admit: and thus respect will often be changed into disgust. Nay, indeed, the superior orders in society do not choose to be too closely copied, in those things which they deem their exclusive privileges; especially by one who, (they must think,) secretly depends on them to defray the expense of the intrusive competition. The consistent minister of Christ will certainly desire to avoid every thing mean and sordid, and to retrench in every other way rather than exhibit the appearance of penury: but, provided he and his family can maintain a decent simplicity, and the credit of punctuality in his payments, he will not think of aspiring any higher. If, in order to do this, he be compelled to exercise considerable self-denial, he will think little of it, while he looks more to Jesus and his Apostles, than to the few of a superior rank who profess the gospel: and could he afford something genteel and fashionable, he would deem it more desirable to devote a larger portion to pious and charitable uses, than to squander it in vain affectation. Perhaps Satan never carried a more important point, within the visible church, than when the opinion was adopted, that *the clergy were gentlemen by profession;* and when he led them to infer from it, *that they and their families ought to live in a genteel and fashionable style.* As the body of the clergy have been mostly but slenderly provided for, when they were thus taught to imitate the appearance of the affluent, the most effectual step was taken to reduce them to abject dependence; to convert them into parasites and flatterers; to render them very indulgent to the vices of the rich and great; or even to tempt them to become the instruments of accomplishing their ambitious and licentious designs; and no small part of the selfishness and artifices of the clergy, which are now made a pretext for abolishing the order, and even for renouncing Christianity, have in fact, originated from this fatal mistake. In proportion as the same principle is adopted by ministers of any description, similar effects will follow; and a degree of dependence, inconsistent with unembarrassed faithfulness, must be the consequence: nor can we in all cases, and without respect of persons, 'declare the whole counsel of God,' unless we be willing, if required, to be, and to appear as, the poor followers of Him 'who had not where to lay his head.'

Then said Christian to Hopeful, Let us not stir a step, but still keep on our way.—Inexperienced believers are very liable to be seduced by the example and persuasions of hypocrites; and to deviate from the direct path, in order to obtain worldly advantages, by means that many men deem fair and honorable. In this case the counsel and warnings of an experienced companion are of the greatest moment.

Especially since the judgment which overtook her, did make her an example within sight of where they are: for they cannot choose but see her, did they but lift up their eyes.—It is indeed most wonderful that men, who profess to believe the Bible, can so confidently attempt to reconcile the love of the world with the service of God; when the instructions, warnings and examples in the sacred volume, which show the fatal consequences of such endeavors, are so numerous, express, and affecting! If Lot's wife, who merely hankered after the possessions she had left behind in Sodom, and looked back with a design of returning, was made a monument of the Lord's vengeance, and a warning to all future ages; what will be the doom of those professed Christians, who habitually prefer worldly gain, or the vain pomp and indulgence that may be purchased with it, to the honor of Christ, and obedience to his most reasonable commandments? The true cause of this infatuation is here assigned: they 'do not lift up their eyes;' and it is to be feared most of them never will, before 'they lift them up in hell, being in torment.'

CHAPTER XV

DOUBTING CASTLE AND GIANT DESPAIR

So when they were disposed to go on, (for they were not as yet at their journey's end,) they ate, and drank, and departed.—When Abraham had given place to his nephew Lot, and receded from his interest for the credit of his religion, he was immediately favored with a most encouraging vision. Thus the Pilgrims, having been enabled to resist the temptations to turn aside for lucre, were indulged with more abundant spiritual consolations. The Holy Spirit, the inexhaustible source of life, light, holiness and joy, is represented by the 'River of God;' even that 'River of the water of life, clear as crystal, proceeding out of the throne of God and the Lamb.' All believers partake of his sacred influences, which prepare the soul for heavenly felicity, and are earnests and pledges of it: but there are seasons when he communicates his holy comforts in larger measure; when the Christian sees such glory in the salvation of Christ; so clearly ascertains his interest in it; and realizes his obligations and privileges, with such lively exercises of adoring love, gratitude and joy, that he is raised above his darkness and difficulties; enjoys sweet communion with God; forgets, for the moment, the pain of former conflicts and the prospect of future trials; finds his inbred corruptions reduced to a state of subjection, and his maladies healed by lively exercises of faith in the divine Savior; and anticipates with unspeakable delight the glory that shall be revealed. Then communion with humble believers, (the lilies that adorn the banks of the river,) is very pleasant; and the soul's rest and satisfaction in God and his service are safe, and his calm confidence is well grounded; being widely different from every species of carnal security. Had this River been intended as the emblem of pardon, justification and adoption, as some understand the passage, it would not have been thus occasionally introduced; for these belong to believers at all times, without any interruption or variation: but the more abundant consolations of the Spirit are not vouchsafed in the same manner, and on them the actual enjoyment of our privileges in a great measure depends.

'Tis according to my wish, said Christian; here is the easiest going; come, good Hopeful, and let us go over.—Believers, even when in the path of duty, walking by faith, and supported by the sanctifying influence of the Spirit, may be abridged of those holy consolations which they have experienced: and if this trial be accompanied with temporal losses, poverty, sickness, the unkindness of friends or ill usage from the world, they may be greatly discouraged; and Satan may have a special advantage in tempting them to discontent, distrust, envy or coveting. Thus, being more disposed to 'wish for a better way,' than to pray earnestly for an increase of faith and patience, they are tempted to look out for some method of declining the cross, or shifting the difficulty which wearies them: nor will it be long before some expedient for a temporary relief will be suggested. The path of duty being rough, a *by-path* is discovered which seems to lead the same way: but, if they will thus turn aside, though they need not break through a hedge, they must go over a stile. The commandments of God mark out the path of holiness and safety: but a deviation from the exact strictness of them may sometimes be plausible, and circumstances may seem to invite to it. Men imagine some providential interposition, giving ease to the weary; and they think that the precept may be interpreted with some latitude, that prudence should be exercised, and that scrupulousness about little things is a mark of *legality* or superstition. Thus by 'leaning to their own understandings,' and 'trusting in their own hearts,' instead of asking counsel of the Lord, they hearken to the tempter. Nor is it uncommon for Christians of deeper experience, and more established reputation to mislead their juniors, by turning aside from the direct line of obedience. For the Lord leaves them to themselves, to repress their self-confidence, and keep them entirely dependent on him; and thus teaches young converts to follow no man further than he follows Christ.

But behold the night came on, and it grew very dark; so that they that went behind lost the sight of him that went before.—It would not be politic in Satan to tempt believers at first to flagrant crimes at which their hearts revolt: and therefore he endeavors to draw them aside, under various pretences, into such plausible deviations as seem to be of no bad repute or material consequence. But every wrong step makes way for further temptations, and serves to render other sins apparently necessary: and if it be a deliberate violation of the least precept in the smallest instance, from carnal motives, it involves such self-will, unbelief, ingratitude, and worldly idolatry, as will most certainly expose the believer to sharp rebukes and painful corrections. The example also of vain pretenders to religion, of whom perhaps, at the first interview, too favorable an opinion has been formed, helps to increase the confidence of him who has departed from the path of obedience: for these men often express the strongest assurance, and venture to violate the precepts of Christ, under pretence of honoring his free-grace, and knowing their liberty and privilege! But darkness must soon envelope all who follow such guides, and the most extreme distress and danger are directly in the way they take.

Fell into a deep pit, which was on purpose there made by the Prince of those grounds, to catch vainglorious fools withal, and was dashed in pieces with his fall.—This circumstance may represent the salutary effects which are sometimes produced on offending believers, by the awful death of some vainglorious hypocrite, to whom they have given too much attention. The Lord, however, will in one way or other deliver his servants from the temporary prevalence of vain-confidence; while presumptuous transgressors perish in the pit of darkness and despair.

Now it began to rain, and thunder, and lighten in a most dreadful manner, and the water rose amain.—The holy law condemns every transgression: when the Christian, therefore, has fallen into wilful sin, he is often led to fear that his faith is dead, that he is still under the law, and that his person as well as his conduct is liable to its righteous condemnation. Thus he is brought back again, as it were, to the tempest, thunder and lightning of mount Sinai.

Let me go first, that, if there be any danger, I may be first therein; because by my means we are both gone out of the way.—This dialogue is very natural and instructive, and exhibits that spirit of mutual tenderness, forbearance, and sympathy, which becomes Christians in such perplexing circumstances. They, who have misled others into sin, should not only ask forgiveness of God, but of them also; and they who have been drawn aside by the example and persuasion of their brethren, should be careful not to upbraid or discourage them, when they become sensible of their fault.

Yet they adventured to go back; but it was so dark, and the flood was so high, that in their going back they had like to have been drowned, nine or ten times.—When such as have turned aside are called upon in Scripture to return to God and his ways, the exhortation implies a promise of acceptance to all who comply with it, and may be considered as immediately addressed to every one with whose character and situation it corresponds. It might be thought, indeed, that an experienced believer, when convinced of any sin, would find little difficulty in returning to his duty and recovering his peace. But a deliberate transgression, however trivial it might seem at the moment, appears upon the retrospect to be an act of most ungrateful and aggravated rebellion; so that it brings such darkness upon the soul, and guilt on the conscience, as frequently causes a man to suspect that all his religion has been a delusion. And, when he would attempt to set out anew, it occurs to him, that if all his past endeavors and expectations, for many years, have been frustrated, he can entertain little hope of better success hereafter; as he knows not how to use other means, or greater earnestness, than he has already employed, as he fears, to no purpose. Nor will Satan ever fail, in these circumstances, to pour in such suggestions as may overwhelm the soul with an apprehension that the case is hopeless, and God inexorable. The believer will not, indeed, be prevailed upon by these discouragements wholly to neglect all attempts to recover his ground: but he often resembles a man who is groping in the dark and cannot find his way, or who is passing through a deep and rapid stream, and struggling hard to keep his head above water.

The giant, therefore, drove them before him, and put them into his castle, into a very dark dungeon, nasty and stinking to the spirits of these two men.—When David had fallen into the depths of sin and distress, he cried most earnestly to the Lord; and Jonah did the same in the fish's belly. Extraordinary cases require singular diligence; even as greater exertion is necessary to get out of a pit than to walk upon level ground. When believers, therefore, have brought themselves, by transgressions, into great terror and anguish of conscience, it is foolish to expect that God will 'restore to them the joy of his salvation,' till they have made the most unreserved confessions of their guilt: humbly deprecated his deserved wrath in persevering prayer, and used peculiar diligence in every thing that accompanies repentance and faith in Christ; and tends to greater watchfulness, circumspection, and self-denial. But they often seek relief in a more compendious way; and, as they do not wholly omit their customary religious exercises, or vindicate and repeat their transgressions; they endeavor to quiet themselves by general notions of the mercy of God through Jesus Christ, and the security of the new covenant; and the storm in their consciences subsiding, they 'find a little shelter,' and 'wait for a more convenient opportunity' of recovering their former life and vigor in religion. Indeed the very circumstances which should excite us to peculiar earnestness, tend, through the depravity of our nature, to blind and stupefy the heart: Peter and the other disciples 'slept for sorrow,' when they were more especially required 'to watch and pray, that they might not enter into temptation.' Such repeated sins and mistakes bring believers into deep distress. Growing more and more heartless in religion, and insensible in a most perilous situation, they are led *habitually* to infer that they are hypocrites; that the encouragements of Scripture belong not to them; that prayer itself will be of no use to them: and, when they are at length brought to reflection, they are taken prisoners by Despair, and shut up in Doubting Castle. This case should be carefully distinguished from Christian's terrors in the City of Destruction, which induced him to 'flee from the wrath to come;' from the Slough of Despond, into which he fell when diligently seeking salvation; from the burden he carried to the cross; from his conflict with Apollyon, and his troubles in the Valley of the Shadow of Death; and even from the terrors that seized him and Hopeful in By-path-meadow, which would have speedily terminated if they had not slept on forbidden ground, and stopped short of the refuge the Lord hath provided. Despair, like a tremendous giant, will at last seize on the souls of all unbelievers: and when Christians conclude, from some aggravated and pertinacious misconduct, that they belong to that company, even their acquaintance with the Scripture will expose them to be taken captive by him. They do not indeed fall and perish with Vain-Confidence: but for a season they find it impossible to rise superior to prevailing gloomy doubts bordering on despair, or to obtain the least comfortable hope of deliverance, or encouragement to use the proper means of seeking it. Whenever we deliberately quit the plain path of duty, to avoid hardship and self-denial, we trespass on Giant Despair's grounds; and are never out of his reach till renewed exercises of deep repentance and faith in Christ, producing unreserved obedience, especially in that instance where before we refused it, have set our feet in the highway we had forsaken. This we cannot attain to, without the special grace of God, which he may not see good immediately to communicate; in the mean time every effort must be accompanied with discouragement and distress: but if, instead of persevering, amidst our anxious fears, to cry to him for help, and wait his time of showing mercy, we endeavor to bolster up some false confidence, and take shelter in a refuge of lies, the event will be such as is here described. It will be in vain, after such perverseness, to pretend that we have inadvertently mistaken our way: 'our own hearts will condemn us;' how then can 'we have confidence toward God, who is greater than our hearts, and knoweth all things?' the grim Giant will prove too strong for us, and shut us up in his noisome dungeon, and the recollection of our former hopes and comforts will only serve to aggravate our wo. These lines are here inserted:—

> 'The Pilgrims now, to gratify the flesh,
> Will seek its ease, but, oh! how they afresh
> Do thereby plunge themselves new griefs into!
> Who seek to please the flesh themselves undo.'

Now in this place Christian had double sorrow, because it was through his unadvised counsel that they were brought into this distress.—Perhaps the exact time, from Wednesday morning till Saturday night, was mentioned, under the idea that it was as long as life can generally be supported in such a situation. The believer may be brought by wilful sin to such a condition that, to his own apprehension, destruction is inevitable. Even a true Christian may sink so low as to have no light or comfort from the Scriptures and the Holy Spirit; nothing to sustain his almost expiring faith and hope; no help or pity from his brethren, but severe censures or more painful suspicions; the horrors of an accusing conscience, the dread of God as an enemy, connected with sharp and multiplied corrections in his outward circumstances; and all this as the price of the ease or indulgence obtained by some wilful transgression! Now who *that really believes this*, will take encouragement to sin from the doctrine of final perseverance? Would a man, for a trivial gain, leap down a precipice, even if he could be sure that he should escape with his life? No, the dread of the anguish of broken bones, and of being made a cripple to the end of his days, would effectually secure him from such a madness.

Wherefore he withdrew, and left them, as before, to consider what to do.—Despair seldom fully seizes any man in this world; and the strongest hold it can get of a true believer amounts only to a prevailing distrust of God's promises, *with respect to his own case:* for this is accompanied by some small degree of latent hope, discoverable in its effects, though unperceived amidst the distressing feelings of the heart. Perhaps this was intended in the allegory by the circumstance of Despair's doing nothing to the Pilgrims, save at the instance of his wife Diffidence. Desponding fears, when they so prevail as to keep men from prayer, make way for temptations to suicide, as the only relief from misery: but when there is any true faith, however it may seem wholly out of exercise, the temptation will be eventually overcome, provided actual insanity do not intervene; and this is a very uncommon case among religious people, whatever slanders their enemies may circulate, in order to prejudice men's minds against the truth. Most, if not all, modern editions read, 'for he sometimes *in sunshiny weather* fell into fits:' but the words *in sunshiny weather*, are not in the old edition before me. If the author afterward added them, he probably intended to represent those transient glimpses of hope, which preserve believers from such dire extremities in their most discouraged seasons.

With these words Hopeful at present did moderate the mind of his brother; so they continued together in the dark that day, in their sad and doleful condition.—They, who have long walked with stable peace in the ways of God, are often known to be more dejected, when sin hath filled their consciences with remorse, than younger professors are; especially if they have caused others to offend, or brought reproach on the gospel. Their recent conduct, as inconsistent with their former character and profession, seems a decided proof of self-deception; they deem it hopeless to begin all over again; Satan endeavors to the utmost to dishearten new converts by their example; and the Lord permits them to be overwhelmed for a time with discouragement, for a warning to others; to vindicate the honor of his truth which they have disgraced; to counter-poise such attainments or services, as might otherwise 'exalt them above measure;' and to show that none has any strength independent of Him, and that he can make use of the feeble to assist the strong, when he sees good. Hopeful's arguments against self-murder are conclusive: doubtless men in general venture on that awful crime, either disbelieving or forgetting the doctrine of Scripture concerning a future and eternal state of retribution. It is greatly to be wished, that all serious persons would avoid speaking of self-murderers, as having *put an end to their existence;* which certainly tends to mislead the mind of the tempted, into very erroneous misapprehensions on this most important subject. This discourse aptly represents the fluctuation of men's minds under great despondency; their struggles against despair, with purposes at some future opportunity to seek deliverance; their present irresolution; and the way in which feeble hopes, and strong fears of future wrath keep them from yielding to the suggestions of the enemy.

Wherefore let us, (at least to avoid the shame that becomes not a Christian to be found in,) bear up with patience as well as we can.—Serious recollection of past conflicts, dangers, and deliverances, is peculiarly useful to encourage confidence in the power and mercy of God, and patient waiting for him in the most difficult and perilous situations: and conference with our brethren, even if they too are under similar trials, is a very important means of resisting the devil, when he would tempt us to renounce our hope, and have recourse to desperate measures.

Make them believe, ere a week comes to an end, thou wilt tear them in pieces, as thou hast done their fellows before them.—The Scripture exhibits some examples of apostates who have died in despair, (as king Saul and Judas Iscariot;) and several intimations are given of those, to whom nothing 'remains but a certain fearful looking for of judgment and fiery indignation.' A few instances also have been recorded in different ages, of notorious apostates, who have died in blasphemous rage and despair. These accord to the man in the iron cage at the house of the Interpreter, and are awful warnings to all professors, 'while they think they stand, to take heed lest they fall.' But the hypocrite generally overlooks the solemn caution; and the humble Christian, having a tender conscience, and an acquaintance with the deceitfulness of his own heart, is very apt to consider his wilful transgression as the unpardonable sin, and to fear, lest the doom of former apostates will at length be his own. This seems intended, by the Giant showing the Pilgrims the bones of those he had slain, in order to induce them to self-murder.

Well, on Saturday, about midnight, they began to pray, and continued in prayer till almost break of day.— Perhaps the author selected 'Saturday at midnight' for the precise time when the prisoners began to pray, in order to intimate, that the return of the Lord's day, and that preparation which serious persons are reminded to make for its sacred services, are often the happy means of recovering those that have fallen into sin and despondency. Nothing will be effectual for the recovering of the fallen, till they 'begin to pray' with fervency, importunity, and perseverance. Ordinary diligence will in this case be unavailing: they have sought ease to the flesh, when they ought to have 'watched unto prayer;' and they must now watch and pray when others sleep: and they must struggle against reluctancy, and persist in repeated approaches to the mercy-seat, till they obtain a gracious answer. But such is our nature and situation, that in proportion as we have special need for earnestness in these devout exercises, our hearts are averse to them. The child, while obedient, anticipates the pleasure of meeting his affectionate parent; but, when conscious of having offended, he, from shame, fear, and pride, hides himself, and keeps at a distance. Thus unbelief, guilt, and a proud aversion to unreserved self-abasement, wrought on by Satan's temptations, keep even the believer, when he has fallen into any aggravated sin, from coming to his only Friend, and availing himself of his sole remedy: 'He keeps silence, though his bones wax old with his roaring all the day long.' (Psalm 32:3–5.) But when stoutness of spirit is broken down, and a contrite believing frame of mind succeeds, the offender begins to cry fervently to God for mercy, with humiliating confessions, renewed application to the blood of Christ, and perseverance amidst delays and discouragements: and then it will not be very long ere he obtain complete deliverance.

Many, therefore, that followed after, read what was written, and escaped the danger.—The promise of eternal life, to every one without exception, who believes in Christ, is especially intended by the key; but without excluding any other of 'the exceeding great and precious promises' of the gospel. The believer, being enabled to recollect such as peculiarly suit his case, and conscious of cordially desiring the promised blessings, has the 'key in his bosom, which will open any lock in Doubting Castle:' and while he pleads the promises in faith, depending on the merits and atonement of Emmanuel, 'coming to God through him;' he gradually resumes his confidence, and begins to wonder at his past despondency. Yet remains of unbelief, recollection of his aggravated guilt, and fear lest he should presume, often render it difficult for him entirely to dismiss discouraging doubts. But let it especially be noted that the faith which delivered the Pilgrims from Giant Despair's castle, induced them without delay to return into the highway of obedience, and to walk in it with more circumspection than before, no more complaining of its roughness; and to devise every method of cautioning others against passing over the stile into By-path-meadow. Whereas a dead faith and a vain confidence keep out all doubts and fears, even on forbidden ground, and under the walls of Despair's castle; till at length the poor deluded wretch is unexpectedly and irresistibly seized upon, and made his prey. And if *Christians* follow Vain-Confidence, and endeavor to keep up their hopes when neglecting their known duty; let them remember, that, (whatever some men may pretend,) they will surely be thus brought acquainted with Diffidence, immured in Doubting Castle, and terribly bruised and frighted by Giant Despair; nor will they be delivered till they have learned, by painful experience, that the assurance of hope is inseparably connected with the self-denying obedience of faith and love.

CHAPTER XVI

THE DELECTABLE MOUNTAINS

Shepherd: These mountains are Emmanuel's Land, and they are within sight of his city; and the sheep also are his, and he laid down his life for them.—When offending Christians are brought to deep repentance, renewed exercises of lively faith, and willing obedience in those self-denying duties which they have declined, the Lord 'restores them the joy of his salvation,' and their former comforts become more abundant and permanent. The Delectable Mountains seem intended to represent those calm seasons of peace and comfort, which consistent believers often experience in their old age. They have survived, in a considerable degree, the vehemence of their youthful passions, and have honorably performed their parts in the active scenes of life: they are established, by long experience, in the simplicity of dependence and obedience: the Lord graciously exempts them from peculiar trials and temptations: their acquaintance with the ministers and people of God is enlarged, and they possess the respect, confidence, and affection of many esteemed friends: they have much leisure for communion with God, and the immediate exercises of religion: and they often converse with their brethren on the loving kindness and truth of the Lord till 'their hearts burn within them.' Thus 'leaning on their staves,' depending on the promises and perfections of God in assured faith and hope, they anticipate their future happiness 'with joy unspeakable and full of glory.' These things are represented under a variety of external images, according to the nature of an allegory. The Shepherds and their flocks denote the more extensive acquaintance of many aged Christians with the ministers and churches of Christ, the Chief Shepherd, 'who laid down his life for the sheep.' This is 'Emmanuel's land;' for, being detached from worldly engagements and connections, they now spend their time almost wholly among the subjects of the Prince of Peace, and as in his more especial presence.

The following lines are added here, as before:—

> 'Mountains delectable they now ascend,
> Where Shepherds be, which to them do commend
> Alluring things, and things that cautions are:
> Pilgrims are steady kept by faith and fear.'

Shepherd: Too far for any but those that shall get thither indeed.—The certainty of the final perseverance of true believers is continually exemplified in their actually persevering, notwithstanding all imaginable inward and outward impediments. Many hold the doctrine who are not interested in the privilege: and whose conduct eventually proves that they 'had no root in themselves:' but the true believer acquires new strength by his very trials and mistakes, and possesses increasing evidence that the new covenant is made with him; for, 'having obtained help of God,' he still 'continues in Christ's word,' and 'abides in him:' and, while temptations, persecutions, heresies, and afflictions, which stumble transgressors and detect hypocrites, tend to quicken, humble, sanctify, and establish him, he may assuredly conclude, that 'he shall be kept by the power of God through faith, unto salvation.'

The Shepherds, I say, whose names were Knowledge, Experience, Watchful, and Sincere, took them by the hand.—These names imply much useful instruction, both to ministers and Christians, by showing them what endowments are most essential to the pastoral office. The attention given to preachers should not be proportioned to the degree of their confidence, vehemence, accomplishments, graceful delivery, eloquence, or politeness; but to that of their *knowledge* of the Scriptures, and of every subject that relates to the glory of God and the salvation of souls; their *experience* of the power of divine truth in their own hearts, of the faithfulness of God to his promises, of the believer's conflicts, difficulties, and dangers, and of the manifold devices of Satan to mislead, deceive, pervert, defile, or harass the souls of men; their *watchfulness* over the people, as their constant business and unremitted care, to caution them against every snare, and to recover them out of every error into which they may be betrayed; and their *sincerity*, as manifested by a disinterested, unambitious, unassuming, patient, and affectionate conduct; by proving that they deem themselves bound to practise their own instructions, and by a uniform attempt to convince the people, that they 'seek not *theirs*, but *them.*'

They have continued to this day unburied, as you see, for an example to others, to take heed how they clamber too high, or how they come too near the brink of this mountain.—Human nature always verges to extremes. In former times the least deviation from an established system of doctrine was reprobated as a *damnable* heresy; and some persons, even at this day, tacitly laying claim to infallibility, deem every variation from their standard an error, and every error inconsistent with true piety. But the absurdity and bad effects of this bigotry having been discovered and exposed, it has become far more common to consider indifference about theological truth, as essential to candor and liberality of sentiment; and to vilify, as narrow-minded bigots, all who 'contend earnestly for the faith once delivered to the saints,' however averse they may be to persecution, or disposed to benevolence towards such as differ from them. Thus the great end for which prophets and apostles were inspired, martyrs shed their blood, and the Son of God himself came into the world and died on the cross, is pronounced a matter of no moment! revelation is virtually rejected! (for we may know, without the Bible, that men ought to be sober, honest, sincere, and benevolent;) and those principles, from which all genuine holiness must arise, are contemned as enthusiasm and foolishness! Some errors may indeed consist with true faith: (for who will say that he is in nothing mistaken?) yet no error is absolutely harmless; all must in one way or other, originate from a wrong state of mind or a faulty conduct, and proportionably counteract the design of revelation: and some are absolutely inconsistent with repentance, humility, faith, hope, love, spiritual worship, and holy obedience, and consequently incompatible with a state of acceptance and salvation. These are represented by 'the hill Error,' and a scriptural specimen is adduced. Professed Christians fall into delusions by indulging self-conceit, vainglory, and curiosity: by 'leaning to their own understandings,' and 'intruding into the things they have not seen, vainly puffed up by their fleshly mind,' and by speculating on subjects which are too deep for them. For the fruit of 'the tree of knowledge,' in respect of religious opinions not expressly revealed, is still forbidden; and men vainly thinking it 'good for food, and a tree to be desired to make one wise;' and desiring 'to be as gods,' understanding and accounting for every thing; fall into destructive heresies, do immense mischief, and become awful examples for the warning of their contemporaries and successors.

Then Christian and Hopeful looked one upon another, with tears gushing out, but yet said nothing to the Shepherds.—Many professors, turning aside from the line of conscientious obedience to escape difficulties, experience great distress of mind; which not being able to endure, they desperately endeavor to disbelieve or pervert all they have learned concerning religion: thus they are blinded by Satan through their despondings, and are given over to strong delusions, as the just punishment of their wickedness. Notwithstanding their profession, and the hopes long formed of them, they return to the company of those who are dead in sin, and buried in worldly pursuits; differing from them merely is a few speculative notions, and being far more hopeless than they. This is not only the case with many, at the first beginning of a religious profession as of Pliable at the Slough of Despond, but with some at every stage of the journey. Such examples may very properly demand our tears of godly sorrow and fervent gratitude; when we reflect on our own misconduct, and the loving kindness of the Lord, who hath made us to differ, by first implanting, and then preserving, faith in our hearts.

Shepherd: Ay, and you will have need to use it when you have it too.—No man can see the heart of another, or *certainly know* him to be a true believer: it is, therefore, proper to warn the most approved persons, 'while they think they stand, to take heed lest they fall.' Such cautions, with the diligence, self-examination, watchfulness and prayer which they excite, are the means of perseverance and establishment to the upright. An event maybe certain in itself, and yet inseparable from the method in which it is to be accomplished; and it may appear very uncertain to the persons concerned, especially if they yield to remissness; so that prayer to the Almighty God for strength,

with continual watchfulness and attention to every part of practical religion, is absolutely necessary to 'the full assurance of
hope unto the end.'

*The remembrance of that last thing that the Shepherds
had shown them made their hands shake; by means of
which impediment they could not look steadily through
the glass.*—Such is the infirmity of our nature, even when in
a measure renovated, that it is almost impossible for us vigorously to exercise one holy affection, without failing in some
other. When we confide in God, with assured faith and hope,
we commonly are defective in reverence, humility, and caution:
on the other hand, a jealousy of ourselves, and a salutary fear
of coming short or drawing back, generally weaken confidence
in God, and interfere with a joyful anticipation of our future
inheritance. But, notwithstanding this deduction, through our
remaining unbelief, such experiences are very advantageous.
'Be not high-minded, but fear:' for 'blesed is he that feareth
always.'

CHAPTER XVII

THE ENCHANTED GROUND

Here, therefore, they met with a very brisk lad that came out of that country, and his name was Ignorance.— Multitudes of ignorant persons entirely disregard God and religion; and others have a show of piety, which is grave, reserved, austere, distant, and connected with contemptuous enmity to evangelical truth. But there are some persons of a sprightly disposition, who are more conceited and vain-glorious than haughty and arrogant: who think well of themselves, and presume on the good opinion of their acquaintance; who are open and communicative, though they expose their ignorance continually; who fancy themselves very religious, and expect to be thought so by others; who are willing to associate with evangelical professors, as if they all meant the same thing; and who do not express contempt or enmity, unless urged to it in self-defense. This description of men seems to be represented by the character next introduced, about which the author has repeatedly bestowed much pains. Christian had soon done with Obstinate and Worldly-wise-man: for such men, being outrageous against the gospel, shun all intercourse with established believers, and little can be done to warn or undeceive them: but brisk, conceited, shallow persons, who are ambitious of being thought religious, are shaken off with great difficulty; and they are continually found among the hearers of the gospel. They often intrude themselves at the most sacred ordinances, when they have it in their power; and sometimes are favorably thought of, till further acquaintance proves their entire ignorance. Pride in one form or another, is the universal fault of human nature; but the frivolous vain-glory of empty talkers differs exceedingly from the arrogance and formal self-importance of Scribes and Pharisees, and arises from a different constitution and education, and other habits and associations. This is the town of Conceit, where ignorance resided. A lively disposition, a weak capacity, a confused judgment, the want of information about religion and almost every other subject, a proportionable blindness to all these defects, and a pert forward self-sufficiency, are the prominent features in this portrait: and if a full purse, secular influence, the ability of conferring favors, and the power to excite fears, be added, the whole receives its highest finishing. With these observations on this peculiar character, and a few hints as we proceed, the plain language of the author on this subject will be perfectly intelligible to the attentive reader.

It is not good, I think, to say so to him all at once; let us pass him by, if you will, and talk to him anon, even as he is "able to bear it."—It is best not to converse much at once with persons of this character: but after a few warnings to leave them to their reflections: for their self-conceit is often cherished by altercations, in which they deem themselves very expert, however disgusting their discourse may prove to others.

Hopeful looked after him, and spied on his back a paper with this inscription, "Wanton professor, and damnable apostate."—The *dark lane* seems to mean a season of prevalent impiety, and of great affliction to the people of God. Here the *impartial* author takes occasion to contrast the character of Ignorance with that of Turn-away. Loose evangelical professors look down with supercilious disdain on those who do not understand the doctrines of grace; and think themselves more enlightened, and better acquainted with the liberty of the gospel, than more practical Christians: but in dark times *wanton professors* often turn out *damnable apostates*, and the detection of their hypocrisy makes them ashamed to show their faces among those believers, over whom they before affected a kind of superiority. When convictions subside, and Christ has not set up his kingdom in the heart, the unclean spirit resumes his former habitation, and 'takes to himself seven other spirits more wicked than himself,' who bind the poor wretch faster than ever in the cords of sin and delusion; so that his last state is more hopeless than the first. Such apostasies make the hearts of the upright to tremble; but a recollection of the nature of Turn-away's profession and confidence gradually removes their difficulties, and they recover their hope, and learn to take heed to themselves.

Guilt, with a great club that was in his hand, struck Little-Faith on the head, and with that blow felled him flat to the ground; where he lay bleeding as one that would bleed to death.—The ensuing episode concerning Little-faith was evidently intended to prevent weak Christians being dismayed by the awful things spoken of hypocrites and apostates. In times of persecution, many who seemed to be religious, openly return into the broad way to destruction; and thus Satan murders the souls of men, by threatening to kill their bodies. This is Dead-man's-lane, leading back to Broadway-gate. All true believers are indeed preserved from drawing back to perdition: but the weak in faith, being *faint-hearted*, and *mistrusting* the promises and faithfulness of God, are betrayed into sinful compliances or negligences; they lie down to sleep when they have special need to watch and be sober; they conceal or perhaps deny their profession, are timid and negligent in duty; or in other respects act contrary to their consciences, and thus contract *guilt*. So that Faint-heart threatens and assaults them; Mistrust plunders them; and Guilt beats them down, and makes them almost despair of life. As the robbery was committed in the *dark lane* before mentioned, this seems to have been the author's *precise* meaning: but any unbelieving fears, that induce men to neglect the means of grace, or to adopt sinful expedients of securing themselves, which on the review bring guilt and terror to their consciences, may also be intended.

Fearing lest it should be one Great Grace, that dwells in the town of Good Confidence, they betook themselves to their heels, and left this good man to shift for himself.—As these robbers represent the *inward* effects of unbelief and disobedience, and not any outward enemies, Great-grace may be the emblem of those believers or ministers, who, having honorably stood their ground, endeavor to restore the fallen in the spirit of meekness; by suitable encouragements. The compassionate exhortations or honorable examples of such eminent Christians keep the fallen from entire despondency, and both tend to bring them to repentance, and to inspire them when penitent, and trembling at the word of God, with some hope of finding mercy and grace in this time of urgent need; which seems to be allegorically represented by the flight of the robbers, when they heard that Great-grace was on the road.

Where he was robbed, and how; who they were that did it, and what he had lost; how he was wounded, and that he hardly escaped with life.—The believer's union with Christ, and the sanctification of the Spirit, sealing his acceptance and rendering him meet for heaven, are his invaluable and unalienable jewels. But he may by sin lose his comforts, and not be able to perceive the evidences of his own safety: and even when again enabled to hope that it will be well with him in the event; he may be so harassed by the recollection of the loss he has sustained, the effects of his misconduct on others, and the obstructions he hath thrown in the way of his own comfort and usefulness, that his future life may be rendered a constant scene of disquietude and painful reflections. Thus the doctrine of the believer's final perseverance is both maintained and guarded from abuse: and it is not owing to a man's own care, but to the Lord's free mercy, powerful interposition, and the engagements of the new covenant, that unbelief and guilt do not rob him of his title to heaven, as well as of his comfort and confidence.

Here, therefore, my brother, is thy mistake.—Many *professors*, meeting with discouragements, give up their religion for the sake of this present world: but, if any thence argue, that true *believers* will copy their example, they show that they are neither well established in judgment, nor deeply acquainted with the nature of the divine life, or the objects of its supreme desires and peculiar fears.

"Above all, take the shield of faith, wherewith ye shall be able to quench all the fiery darts of the wicked."—Young converts often view temptations, conflicts, and persecutions, in a very different light than experienced believers do. Warm with zeal, and full of confidence, which they imagine to be wholly genuine, and knowing comparatively little of their own hearts, or the nature of the Christian conflict, they resemble new recruits, who are apt to boast what great things they will do: but the old disciple, though much stronger in faith, and possessing habitually more vigor of holy affection, knows himself too well to boast, and speaks with modesty of the past, and

diffidence of the future; like the veteran soldier, of approved valor, who has often been in actual service. They, who have boasted beforehand what they would do and suffer, rather than deny the faith, have generally either proved apostates, or been taught their weakness by painful experience. And when a real believer has thus fallen, the recollection of past boastings adds to his remorse and terror; and Satan will attempt to drive him to despair: so that, indeed, 'no man can tell what in such a combat attends us, but he that has been in the battle himself.' Even they, who were most remarkable for strength of faith, have often been overcome in the hour of temptation; and, when guilt got within them, they found it no easy matter to recover their hope and comfort: how then can the weak in faith be expected to overcome in such circumstances! The *accommodation* of the passages from Job to this conflict, seems merely intended to imply, that the assaults of Satan on these occasions, are more terrible than any thing in the visible creation can be: and that every possible advantage will be needful in order to withstand in the evil day.

But without him, the proud helpers fall under the slain.—Instead of saying, 'though all men deny thee, yet will not I,' it behoves us to use all means of grace diligently; and to be instant in prayer, that the Lord himself may protect us by his power, and animate us by his presence; and then only shall we be enabled to overcome both the fear of man, and the temptations of the devil.

'Tis true, they rescued were; but yet, you see, They're scourged to boot: let this your caution be.—This way, which *seemed as straight as the right way*, and in entering on which there was no *stile to climb over*, must denote some very plausible and gradual deviation from the simplicity of the gospel, in doctrine or practice. Peculiar circumstances may require the believer to act; while so much can be said in support of different measures, as to make him hesitate: and if he merely consider the subject in his own mind, or consult with his friends, without carefully examining the Scripture, and praying for divine direction, he will very probably be seduced into the wrong path: and, if he listen to the Flatterer, he will certainly be misled. But what is meant by the Flatterer? It cannot reasonably be supposed that the author meant to state that the Pilgrims hearkened to such as preach justification by the works of the law; or

flatter men's self-complacency by harangues on the dignity of human nature, and the unbiassed freedom of the will, the sufficiency of reason in matters of religion, or the goodness of the heart: for experienced Christians cannot be thus imposed on. And gross antinomianism can never greatly attract the attention of those, who have been in Doubting Castle for turning aside into By-path-meadow. But the human mind is always accessible to flattery, in one form or other; and there have in every age been teachers and professed Christians, who have soothed men into a good opinion of their state on insufficient grounds; or fed their spiritual pride by expressing too favorable thoughts of their attainments, which is often mistaken for a very loving spirit. This directly tends to induce unwatchfulness, and an unadvised way of deciding in difficult cases: and thus men are imperceptibly led to consult their own inclination, ease, or interest, instead of the will and glory of God. In the mean time, such flatterers commend their prudence, in allowing themselves a little rest; persuade them that they are entitled to distinction, and exempted from general rules; insinuate, that they are too well acquainted with Satan's devices, to be deceived; and in short seem to make their opinion the standard of right and wrong. Some excellent men, from a natural easiness of temper, united with spiritual love and genuine candor, thus *undesignedly* too much soothe their brethren: but the Flatterer is '*a black man in a white robe,*' a designing hypocrite, who, with plausibility, fluency of speech, talents, eloquence, or polite accomplishments, and very evangelical views of religion, 'serves not our Lord Jesus Christ, but his own belly; and by good words and fair speeches deceives the hearts of the simple.' Such a man will not shock serious minds by gross antinomianism: but he will insist disproportionately and indiscriminately on privileges, promises, and consolatory topics; and thus put his auditors into good humor with themselves, and consequently with him, in order to obtain advantages, not so easily acquired by other means. There are many other *flatterers:* but this description, coming far more in the way of evangelical professors than any other, seems emphatically to be intended. Satan aims to lull men into a fatal security, wholly or in part; flatterers of every kind are his principal agents; and a smooth undistinguishing gospel, and want of plain-dealing in private, have immense influence in this respect. Too often, it is to be feared, the preacher uses flattery in the pulpit and the parlor, and is reciprocally flattered or rewarded: and what wonder is it, if ungodly men take up the business as a lucrative trade, and serve their own selfish purposes, by quieting uneasy consciences into a false peace, misleading unwary souls, entangling incautious believers in a net, and thus bringing a scandal on the gospel? 'Satan is transformed into an angel of light, and his ministers into ministers of righteousness;' and if this were the case in the apostles' days, in the midst of terrible persecutions, it may well be expected, that the same attempts will be made at other times. Among persons not much acquainted with the gospel, a different method of seduction will be employed; in some places by vain philosophy or pharisaical self-righteousness, in others by enthusiastic imaginations or dreams of sinless perfection: but among established Christians, some plausible scheme, flattering men as wise and strong in Christ, and as knowing their liberty and privileges, must be adopted; such as were propagated among the Corinthians, or those professed Christians whom James, Peter, and Jude successively addressed. In the present state of religious profession, a more important caution, I apprehend, cannot be given by the united voice of all those ministers, whom the Shepherds represent, than this, 'Beware of the Flatterer;' of all teachers who address the self-preference of the human heart, and thus render men forgetful of 'taking heed to their way according to the word of God.' For if men overlook the precepts of Scripture, and forsake practical distinguishing preachers, to follow such as bolster up their hopes in an unscriptural manner, they will either be fatally deceived, or drawn out of the path of truth and duty, taken in the net of error, and entangled among injurious connections and with perplexing difficulties. They will indeed at length be undeceived as to these *fine-spoken men*, but not till they scarcely know what to do or what will become of them. For when the Lord plucks their feet out of the net, he will humble them in the dust for their sin and folly; and make them thankful to be delivered, though with severe rebukes and corrections.

So they turned away from the man; and he, laughing at them, went his way.—Some false professors gradually renounce 'the truth as it is in Jesus:' but others openly set themselves against all kinds of religion, and turn scoffers and infidels. Indeed none are more likely to become avowed atheists, than such as have for many years hypocritically professed the gospel; for they often acquire an acquaintance with the several parts of religion, their connection with each other, and the arguments with which they are supported; so that they know not where to begin, if they would oppose any particular doctrine or precept of revelation. Yet they hate the whole system; and, having never experienced those effects from the truth, which the Scripture ascribes to it, they feel, that if there be any reality in religion, their own case is very dreadful, and wish to shake off this mortifying and alarming conviction. And, as they have principally associated with loose professors, and witnessed much folly and wickedness among them, they willingly take up a bad opinion of all who pretend to piety, (as rakes commonly revile all women,) and so they make a desperate plunge, and treat the whole of religion as imposture and delusion; pretending, that upon a thorough investigation, they find it to be a compound of knavery, folly and fanaticism. Thus God in awful judgment permits Satan to blind their eyes, because they 'obeyed not the truth, but had pleasure in unrighteousness.' Men set out with a dead faith and a worldly heart, and at length occupy the seat of the scorner! The vain reasonings and contemptuous sneers of such apostates, may turn aside other unsound characters, and perplex new converts; but the experience of established believers will fortify them against these manifest delusions; and corrections for previous mistakes will render them jealous of themselves and one another; so that they will go on their way with greater circumspection, and pity the scorner who ridicules them.

Hitherto hath thy company been my mercy; and thou shalt have a good reward for thy labor.—The Enchanted Ground may represent a state of exemption from peculiar trials, and of worldly prosperity; especially when Christians unexpectedly advanced in their outward circumstances, or engaged in extensive, flourishing business. A concurrence of agreeable dispensations sometimes succeeds to long continued difficulties; the believer's peace is little interrupted, but he has not very high affections or consolations; he meets with respect and attention from his friends and acquaintance; and is drawn on by success in his secular undertakings. This powerfully tends, through remaining depravity, to produce a lethargic and indolent frame of mind: the man attends on religious ordinances,

and the constant succession of duties, more from habit and conscience, than from delight in the service of God: and even they,
who have acquitted themselves creditably in a varied course of
trials and conflicts, often lose much of their vigor, activity and
vigilance, in these fascinating circumstances. No situation, in
which a believer can be placed, requires so much watchfulness:
other experiences resemble storms, which keep a man awake
almost against his will; this is a treacherous calm, which
invites and lulls him to sleep. But pious discourse, the jealous
cautions of faithful friends, and recollections of the Lord's dealings with us in times past, are admirably suited to counteract
this tendency. The subsequent dialogue contains the author's
own exposition of several particulars in the preceding allegory.

*Christian: And could you at any time, with ease, get
off the guilt of sin, when by any of these ways it came
upon you?*—This word is used here and in other places, not to
signify *the evil of sin in the sight of God,* and the transgressor's
deserved liableness to punishment: but the *remorse and fear
of wrath,* with which the convinced sinner is oppressed, and
from which he often seeks relief by means which exceedingly
increase his actual guilt. Nothing except a free pardon, by faith
in the atoning sacrifice of Christ, can take away *guilt:* but the
uneasiness of a man's conscience may be for a time removed by
various expedients. The words *guilt* or *guilty,* are often used in
this latter sense, by modern divines; but it does not seem to be
scripturally accurate, and may produce misapprehensions.

*And now was my heart full of joy, mine eyes full of
tears, and mine affections running over with love to the
name, people, and ways of Jesus Christ.*—Coming to Christ
is properly the *effect of faith:* yet the language here used is
warranted by Scripture. The word *reveal,* and the vision of
Christ conversing with Hopeful, *seem* to sanction such things
as have been greatly mistaken and abused, and have occasioned many scandals and objections: yet it is evident, that the
author meant nothing contrary to the most sober statement
of scriptural truth. Christ did not appear to Hopeful's *senses,*
but to his *understanding:* and the words spoken are no other
than texts of Scripture taken in their genuine meaning; not
informing him, as by a new revelation, that his sins were pardoned, but encouraging him to apply for this mercy and all
other blessings of salvation. So that, (allowing for the nature

of an allegory,) the whole account for substance exactly coincides with the experience of the most sober Christians; who, having been deeply humbled, and ready to sink under discouragement, have had such views of the love of Christ, of his glorious salvation, the freeness of the invitations, the largeness of the promises, and the nature of justifying faith, as have 'filled them with peace and joy in believing:' and these have been followed by such abiding effects as are here described, which completely distinguish them from all the false joys of hypocrites and enthusiasts. Others indeed cannot relate so orderly an account of their convictions and comforts; yet they are brought, (though by varied methods,) to the same reliance on Christ and the same devoted obedience.

CHAPTER XVIII

IGNORANCE

How stands it between God and your soul now?—In this dialogue Ignorance speaks exactly in character; and the answers of the Pilgrims are conclusive against such absurd and unscriptural grounds of confidence, as are continually maintained by many who would be thought pious Christians.

Ignorance: But I think of them, and desire them.—The desire of heavenly felicity, when the real nature of it is not understood, the proper means of obtaining it are neglected, other objects are preferred to it, or sloth and procrastination intervene, is no proof that a man will be saved. In like manner this expression, *the desire of grace is grace,* must be owned to be very fallacious and ambiguous. Men may be notionally convinced, that without grace they must perish, and mere selfishness may excite some feeble desires after it; though worldly affections predominate, and the real value of the spiritual good is not perceived. But to hunger and thirst for God and his righteousness, his favor, image, and service, as the supreme good; so that no other object can satisfy the earnest desire of the heart, and every thing is renounced that interferes with the pursuit of it, is grace indeed, and shall be completed in glory.

Christian: That may be through its deceitfulness; for a man's heart may minister comfort to him in the hopes of that thing, for which he has yet no ground to hope.—It is exceedingly dangerous to make comfort a ground of confidence; unless the nature, source, and effects of that comfort be considered: for it may result entirely from ignorance and self-flattery, in a variety of ways.

"There is none righteous, there is none that doeth good."—'That which is born of the flesh, is flesh;' 'The carnal mind is enmity against God; for it is not subject to the law of God, neither indeed can be. So then they that are in the flesh cannot please God;' for 'They are *by nature* the children of wrath.' This is man's *natural* condition: but of the regenerate it is said, 'Ye are not in the flesh, but in the Spirit;' 'for that which is born of the Spirit, is Spirit:' and to such persons the texts adduced do not apply.

All our righteousness stinks in his nostrils, and that therefore he cannot abide to see us stand before him in any confidence, even in all our best performances.—The external services, performed by unregenerate persons from selfish motives, being scanty and partial, and made the ground of self-complacency, and self-righteous pride, 'are abomination in the sight of God,' however 'highly esteemed among men:' 'For men look at the outward appearance, but the Lord looketh at the heart.' Even the obedience of a true believer, though it springs from right principles, and has some spiritual excellency in it, is yet so defective and defiled by sin, that if it were not accepted as the fruit of the Spirit through the mediation of Christ, it must be condemned by the holy law, and rejected with abhorrence by a God of infinite purity. Men may allow this in words, and yet not know what it is to come as condemned sinners, for a free justification and salvation, by faith in Christ.

This faith maketh not Christ a justifier of thy person, but of thy actions; and of thy person for thy actions' sake, which is false.—The way of being justified by faith, for which Ignorance pleads, may well be called *'fantastical,'* as well as *'false;'* for it is no where laid down in Scripture: and it not only changes the way of acceptance, but it takes away the rule and standard of righteousness, and substitutes a vague notion, called *sincerity*, in its place, which never was, or can be, defined with precision.

That he cannot by any man be savingly known, unless God the Father reveals him to him.—Pride, unbelief, and carnal prejudices or affections, so close the mind of a sinner against the spiritual glory of the Person and redemption of Christ, that nothing but the illumination of the Spirit removing this veil can enable him to understand and receive the revelation of the sacred oracles on these important subjects.

If there be so many in our parts, how many, think you, must there be in the place where he was born?—If numbers of ignorant persons may be found among the apparently religious, what must be the case of those, who are left without instruction to their native pride and self-conceit!

To any thing that may dishonor God, break its peace, grieve the Spirit, or cause the enemy to speak reproachfully.—Fears of wrath are too generally ascribed to unbelief, and deemed prejudicial; but this arises from ignorance and mistake; for belief of God's testimony must excite fears in every heart, till it is clearly perceived how that wrath maybe escaped; and doubts mingled with hopes must arise from faith, till a man is conscious of having experienced a saving change. These fears and doubts excite men to self-examination, watchfulness, and diligence; and thus tend to the believer's establishment, and 'the full assurance of hope unto the end:' while the want of them often results from unbelief and stupidity of conscience, and terminates in carnal security and abuse of the gospel. Fears may indeed be excessive and unreasonable, and the effect of unbelief: but it is better to mark the extreme, and caution men against it, than by declaiming indiscriminately against all doubts and fears, to help sinners to deceive themselves, and discourage weak believers from earnestly using the scriptural means of 'making their calling and election sure.'

They see that those fears tend to take away from them their pitiful old self-holiness.—The expression *pitiful old self-holiness*, denotes the opinion that ignorant persons entertain of their *hearts* as good and holy: while the term, *self-righteousness*, relates to their supposed good *lives:* but nothing can be further from our author's meaning, than to speak against 'sanctification by the Spirit unto obedience,' as evidential of our union with Christ, and acceptance in his righteousness.

All of a sudden he grew acquainted with one Save-self, and then he became a stranger to me.—Temporary was doctrinally acquainted with the gospel, but a stranger to its sanctifying power. Such men *have been* forward in religion, but that is now past; for they were always *graceless*, and came short of honesty in their profession, if not in their moral conduct, and were ever ready to *turn back* into the world at a convenient season. They have indeed been alarmed; but terror without humiliation will never subvert self-confidence: and of the numbers with whom some ministers converse under trouble of conscience, and of whom they hope well, how many disappoint their expectations, and after a time plunge deeper into sin than ever! Such convictions resemble the blossoms of the fruit-tree, which must precede the ripe fruit, but do not always produce it: so that we cannot say, 'The more blossoms there are, the greater abundance will there be of fruit;' though we may be assured that there can be no fruit, if there be no blossoms. The reasons and the manner of such men's declensions and apostasy are very justly and emphatically stated: though perhaps not with sufficient delicacy to suit the taste of this fastidious age.

Thus, being launched again into the gulf of misery, unless a miracle of grace prevent it, they everlastingly perish in their own deceivings.—'The hypocrite will not pray always;' nor can he ever pray with faith or sincerity, for spiritual blessings: but he may deprecate misery, and beg to be made happy, and continue to observe a form of private religion. But when such men begin to shun the company of lively Christians, to neglect public ordinances, and to excuse their own conduct, by imitating the devil, the accuser of the brethren, in calumniating pious persons, magnifying their imperfections, insinuating suspicions of them, and aiming to confound all distinction of character among men; we may safely conclude their state to be perilous in the extreme. While professed Christians should be exhorted carefully to look to themselves, and to watch against the first incursions of this spiritual declension; it should also be observed, that the lamented infirmities and dulness of those who persist in using the means of grace, and striving against sin: who decidedly prefer the company of believers, and deem them the excellent of the earth, and who are severe in judging themselves, but candid to others, are of a contrary nature and tendency to the steps of Temporary's apostasy.

CHAPTER XIX

THE LAND OF BEULAH

Here all the inhabitants of the country called them, "the holy people, the redeemed of the Lord, sought out."—The word Beulah signifies *married;* and the prophet, in the passage whence it is quoted, predicted a very flourishing state of religion, which is yet in futurity: but the author accommodates it to the sweet peace and confidence which tried believers commonly experience towards the close of their lives. This general rule admits indeed of exceptions: but the author, having witnessed many of these encouraging scenes, was willing to animate himself and his afflicted brethren with the hope of similar triumphant joy. The communion of saints in prayer, praises, and thanksgivings, with liberty and ardor, and hearts united in cordial love; the beauties of holiness, and the consolations of the Holy Spirit; the healing beams of the Sun of Righteousness, shining by the sweet light of divine truth upon the soul; exemption from darkening temptations and harassing doubts; lively earnests and near prospects of heavenly felicity; a cheering sense of communion with the heavenly host, in their fervent adorations, and a realizing apprehension of their ministering care over the heirs of salvation; a comfortable renewal of the acceptance of Christ, sealed with the tokens, pledges, and assurances of his love; gratitude, submission, confidence in God, hope, and the sweet exercise of tenderness, sympathy, meekness, and humility, but little interrupted by the working of the contrary evils:—these things seem to constitute the happy state here represented. It is remarkable that the Psalms (which were intended, among other uses, to regulate the devotions and experiences of believers) abound at first with confessions, complaints, fears, and earnest cries of distress or danger; but towards the close become more and more the language of confidence, gratitude and joy, and conclude with unmingled praises and thanksgivings.

Wherefore here they lay by it a while, crying out because of their pangs, "If you see my beloved, tell him that I am sick of love."—In the immediate view of heavenly felicity, Paul 'desired to depart hence and be with Christ, as far better' than life; and David 'fainted for God's salvation.' In the lively exercise of holy affections, the believer grows weary of this sinful world; and longs to have his faith changed for sight, his hope swallowed up in enjoyment, and his love perfected, and secured from all interruption and abatement. Were this frame of mind habitual, it might unfit men for the common concerns of life, which appear very trifling to the soul when employed in delightful admiring contemplation of heavenly glory.

It is the nature of the fruit of the grapes of these vineyards, "to go down so sweetly as to cause the lips of them that are asleep to speak."—Attendance on the public ordinances is always the believer's duty and privilege; yet he cannot at all times delight in them: but, when holy affections are in lively exercise, he sweetly rests in these earnests of heavenly joy; and speaks freely and fervently of the love of Christ and the blessings of salvation, to the edification of those around him; who often wonder at witnessing such a change, from reserve and diffidence to boldness and earnestness, in urging others to mind the one thing needful.

Then said the men that met them, You have but two difficulties more to meet with, and then you are in the City.—Perhaps the author here alluded to those pre-intimations of death, that some persons seem to receive: and he appears to have ascribed them to the guardian angels, watching over every believer. *Death*, and *admission into the City,* were the only difficulties that awaited the Pilgrims.

He was much in the troublesome thoughts of the sins that he had committed, both since and before he began to be a pilgrim.—Death is aptly represented by a deep river without a bridge, separating the believer from his heavenly inheritance: as Jordan flowed between Israel and the promised land. From this river, nature shrinks back, even when faith, hope, and love, are in lively exercise; but when these decline, alarm and consternation may unite with reluctance at the thoughts of crossing it. The dreaded pangs that precede the awful separation of those intimate associates, the soul and body; the painful parting with dear friends and every earthly object; the gloomy ideas of the dark, cold, and noisome grave; and the solemn thought of launching into an unseen eternity, render Death the *king of terrors*. But faith in a crucified, buried, risen, and ascended Savior; experience of his faithfulness and love in times past; hope of an immediate entrance into his presence, where temptation, conflicts, sin and suffering will find no admission; and the desire of perfect knowledge, holiness and felicity, will reconcile the mind to the inevitable stroke, and sometimes give a complete victory over every fear. Yet if faith and hope be weakened, through the recollection of any peculiar misconduct, the withholding of divine light and consolation, or some violent assault of the tempter, even the *believer* will be peculiarly liable to alarm and distress. His reflecting mind, having been long accustomed to consider the subject in its important nature and consequences, has very different apprehensions of God, of eternity, of judgment, of sin, and of himself, than other men have. Sometimes experienced saints are more desponding in these circumstances than their junior brethren: constitution has considerable effect upon the mind; and some men (like Christian) are in every stage of their profession, more exposed to temptations of a discouraging nature, than to ambition, avarice, or fleshly lusts. It has before been suggested, that the author probably meant to describe the peculiarities of his own experience, in the character of Christian; and he may perhaps here have intimated his apprehension, lest he should not meet death with becoming fortitude. A conscientious life indeed is commonly favored with a peaceful close, even when forebodings to the contrary have troubled men during their whole lives: and this is so far *general*, that they best provide for a comfortable death, who most diligently attend to the duties of their station, and the improvement of their talents, from evangelical principles; whereas they who live negligently, and yield to temptation, make, as it were, an assignation with terror to meet them on their death-bed, a season when comfort is more desirable than at any other. The Lord, however, is no man's debtor: none can claim consolation as their due: and, though a believer's experience and the testimony of his conscience may evidence the sincerity of his faith and love, yet he must disclaim to the last every other dependence than the righteousness and blood of Christ, and the free mercy of God in him.

Christian therefore presently found ground to stand upon, and so it followed that the rest of the river was but shallow: thus they got over.—The temporary distresses of dying believers often arise from bodily disease, which interrupt the free exercise of their intellectual powers. Of this Satan will be sure to take advantage, as far as he is permitted; and will suggest gloomy imaginations, not only to distress them, but to dishearten others by their example. What may in this state be painted before the fancy we cannot tell: but it is generally observed, that such painful conflicts terminate in renewed hope and comfort, frequently by means of the conversation and prayers of Christians and ministers; so that they, who for a time have been most distressed, have at length died most triumphantly.

They therefore went up through the region of the air, sweetly talking as they went, being comforted, because they safely got over the river, and had such glorious companions to attend them.—When Lazarus died, he was carried by angels into Abraham's bosom; and we have every reason to believe, that the services of these friendly spirits to the souls of departed saints are immediate and sensible; and that their joy is such as is here described. The beautiful description that follows admits of no elucidation: some of the images indeed are taken from modern customs; but in all other respects it is entirely scriptural, and very intelligible and animating to the spiritual mind.

"Blessed are they that do his commandments, that they may have right to the tree of life, and may enter in through the gates into the city."—The commandments of God, as given to sinners under a dispensation of mercy, call them to repentance, faith in Christ, and the obedience of faith and love; the believer habitually practises according to these commandments, from the time of his receiving Christ for salvation; and this evidences his interest in all the blessings of the new covenant, and proves that he has a right through grace to the heavenly inheritance. May the writer of these remarks, and every reader, have such 'an abundant entrance,' as is here

described, 'into the everlasting kingdom of our Lord and Savior Jesus Christ!'

But commanded the two shining ones, that conducted Christian and Hopeful to the City, to go out, and take Ignorance, and bind him hand and foot, and have him, away.—We frequently hear of persons that have lived strangers to evangelical religion, and the power of godliness, dying with great composure and resignation: and such instances are brought forward as an objection to the necessity of faith, or of a devoted life. But what do they prove? What evidence is there, that such men are saved? Is it not far more likely that they continued to the end under the power of ignorance and self-conceit; that Satan took care not to disturb them; and that God gave them over to a strong delusion, and left them to perish with a lie in their right hand? Men, who have neglected religion all their lives, or have habitually for a length of years disgraced an evangelical profession, being when near death visited by pious persons, sometimes obtain a sudden and extraordinary measure of peace and joy, and die in this frame. This should in general be considered as a bad sign: for deep humiliation, yea distress, united with some trembling hope in God's mercy through the gospel, is far more suited to their case, and more likely to be the effect of spiritual illumination. But when a formal visit from a minister of any sect, a few general questions, and a prayer, (with or without the sacrament,) calm the mind of a dying person, whose life has been unsuitable to the Christian profession; no doubt, could we penetrate the veil, we should see him wafted across the River in the boat of Vain-hope, and meeting with the awful doom that is here described. From such delusions, good Lord, deliver us. Amen.

PART II · CHAPTER I

CHRISTIANA

Now, having taken up my lodging in a wood, about a mile off the place, as I slept, I dreamed again.—It has been before observed, that the first part of 'The Pilgrim's Progress' is in all respects the most complete. Yet there are many things in the second well worthy of the pious reader's attention; nor can there be any doubt, but it was penned by the same author. It is not, however, necessary, that the annotator should be so copious upon it, as upon the more interesting instructions of the preceding part. In general, the leading incidents may be considered as the author's own exposition of his meaning in the former part; or as his delineation of some varieties, that occur in events of a similar nature: yet some particulars will demand, and richly deserve, a more full and exact elucidation.

He will look upon all as if done unto himself: and no marvel, for it was for the love that he had to his Prince that he ventured as he did.—Christians are the representatives on earth of the Savior and Judge of the world; and the usage they meet with, whether good or bad, commonly originates in men's love to him, or contemptuous enmity against him. The decisions of the great day therefore will be made, with an especial reference to this evidence of men's faith or unbelief. Faith works by love of Christ, and of his people for his sake, which influences men to self-denying kindness towards the needy and distressed of the flock. Where these fruits are totally wanting, it is evident there is no love of Christ, and consequently no faith in him, or salvation by him. And as true believers are the excellent of the earth, no man can have any good reason for despising, hating, and injuring them; so that this usage will be adduced as a proof of positive enmity to Christ, and expose the condemned sinner to more aggravated misery. Indeed, it often appears after the death of consistent Christians, that the consciences of their most scornful opposers secretly favored them: it must then surely be deemed the wisest conduct by every reflecting person, to 'let these men alone, lest haply he should be found to fight against God.'

Then they all wept again, and cried out, Oh! wo worth the day!—It is here evident, that the author was intent on encouraging pious persons to persevere in using all means for the spiritual good of their children, even when they see no effects produced by them. The Scripture teaches us to expect a blessing on such endeavors: the dying testimony and counsels of exemplary believers frequently make a deeper impression than all their previous instructions: the death of near relations, who have behaved well to such as despised them, proves a heavier loss than was expected: the recollection of unkind behavior to such valuable friends, and of the pains taken to harden the heart against their affectionate admonitions, sometimes lies heavy on the conscience; and thus the prayers of the believer for his children or other relatives, are frequently answered after his death. And when some of them begin to inquire, 'What must we do to be saved?' these will become zealous instruments in seeking the conversion of those, whom before they endeavored to prejudice against the ways of God.

We must, by one way or other, seek to take her off from the thoughts of what shall be hereafter, else all the world cannot help but she will become a pilgrim.—The mind, during sleep, is often occupied about those subjects that have most deeply engaged the waking thoughts: and it sometimes pleases God to make use of ideas thus suggested, to influence the conduct by exciting fears or hopes. Provided an intimation be scriptural, and the effect salutary, we need not hesitate to consider it as a divine monition, however it was brought to the mind; but, if men attempt to draw conclusions in respect of their *acceptance* or *duty;* to determine the truth of certain doctrines; to prophesy, or to discover hidden things, by dreams or visions of any kind: they then become a very dangerous and disgraceful species of enthusiasm. Whatever means are employed, conviction of sin and a disposition earnestly to cry for mercy, are the work of the Holy Spirit in the heart; and on the other hand, the powers of darkness will surely use every effort and stratagem to take off inquirers from thus earnestly seeking the salvation of God.

Sir, will you carry me and my children with you, that we also may go and worship the King?—'The secret of the Lord is with them that fear him.' The intimations given by Secret seem to represent the silent teaching of the Holy Spirit, by which the true meaning of the Scriptures is discovered, and the real grounds of encouragement brought to the penitent's notice or recollection. Thus he learns that the way of salvation is yet open to him: and the invitations of the gospel prove more fragrant and refreshing than the most costly ointment, and more precious than the gold of Ophir. It is observable that Secret did not inform Christiana that her sins were forgiven, or that Christ and the promises belonged to her; but merely that she *was invited to come*, and that coming in the appointed way she would be accepted, notwithstanding her pertinacious unbelief in the preceding part of her life. Thus, without seeming to have intended it, the author hath stated the scriptural *medium* between the extremes which have been contended for with great eagerness and immense mischief in *modern* days; while some maintain, that sinners should not be invited to come to Christ, or commanded to repent and believe the gospel; and others that they should be urged to believe at once, with full assurance, that all the blessings of salvation belong to them, even previously to repentance, or works meet for repentance!

Thou must through troubles, as did he that went before thee, enter this Celestial City.—'Through much tribulation we must enter into the kingdom of God!' Habitual self-denial, even in things lawful in themselves, yet in many cases inexpedient, mortification of our sinful inclinations, inward conflicts, the renunciation of worldly interests and connections, the scorn and hatred of the world, sore temptations, and salutary chastisements, are very bitter to our natural feelings. Habits likewise, and situation, often render some of them extremely painful, like 'cutting off a right-hand, or plucking out a right eye:' and deep poverty, persecution, or seasons of public calamity, may enhance these tribulations. If a man, therefore, meet with nothing *bitter*, in consequence of his religious profession, he has great reason to suspect that he is not in the narrow way;

yet many argue against themselves, on account of those very trials, which are a favorable token in their behalf. But, on the other hand, the believer has 'a joy that a stranger intermeddleth not with,' which counterbalances all his sorrows so that even in this life he possesses more solid satisfaction than they do, who choose the road to destruction from fear of the difficulties attending the way of life. Satan is, however, peculiarly successful in persuading men, that religion, the very essence of heavenly happiness, will make them miserable on earth; and that sin, the source of all the misery in the universe, will make them happy! By such manifest lies does this old murderer support his cause!

I will yet have more talk with this Christiana; and, if I find truth and life in what she shall say, myself with my heart shall also go with her.—The very things which excite the rage and scorn of some persons, penetrate the hearts and consciences of others. Thus the Lord makes one to differ from another, by preparing the heart to receive the good seed of divine truth, which is sown in it; yet every one *willingly chooses* the way he takes, without any constraint or hindrance, except his own prevailing dispositions. This consideration gives the greatest encouragement to the use of all proper means, in order to influence sinners to choose the good part: for who knows but the most obvious truth, warning, or exhortation, given in the feeblest manner, may reach the conscience of a child, relative, neighbor, enemy, or even persecutor; when the most convincing and persuasive discourses of eloquent and learned teachers have failed to produce any effect.

I dare say, my lady herself is an admirable well-bred gentlewoman, and Mr. Lechery is a pretty fellow.—This dialogue, by the names, arguments and discourse introduced into it, shows what kind of persons they in general are, who despise and revile all those that fear God and seek the salvation of their souls; from what principles, affections, and conduct, such opposition springs; and on what grounds it is maintained. Men of the most profligate characters, who never studied or practised religion in their lives, often pass sentence on the sentiments and actions of pious persons, and decide in the most difficult controversies, without the least hesitation; as if they knew the most abstruse subjects by instinct or intuition, and were acquainted with the secrets of men's hearts!

These presumers should consider, that *they* must be wrong, let who will be right; that any religion is as good as open impiety and profligacy; and that it behoves them to 'cast out the beam out of their own eye,' before they attempt 'to pull out the mote from their brother's eye.' Believers also, recollecting the vain conversation from which they have been redeemed, and the obligations that have been conferred upon them, should not disquiet themselves about the scorn and censure of such persons, but learn to pray for them, as entitled to their compassion, even more than their detestation.

PART II · CHAPTER II

THE WICKET-GATE

Yet we will have all things in common betwixt thee and me: only go along with me.—There are remarkable circumstances attending the conversion of some persons, with which others are wholly unacquainted. The singular dispensations of Providence, and the strong impressions made by the word of God upon their minds, seem in their own apprehension almost to amount to a *special* invitation: whereas others are gradually and gently brought to think on religious subjects, and to embrace the proposals of the gospel, who are therefore sometimes apt to conclude, that they have never been truly awakened to a concern about their souls: and this discouragement is often increased by the discourse of such religious characters, as lay great stress on the *circumstances* attending conversion. These misapprehensions, however, are best obviated, by showing that 'the Lord delighteth in mercy;' that Christ 'will in no wise cast out any that come to him;' and that they who leave all earthly pursuits to seek salvation, and renounce all other confidence to trust in the mercy of God through the redemption of his Son, shall assuredly be saved.

Many there be that pretend to be the King's laborers, and that say they are for mending the King's highways, and that bring dirt and dung instead of stone, and so mar, instead of mending.—The author seems to have observed a declension of evangelical religion, subsequent to the publication of his original Pilgrim. Probably he was grieved to find many renounce or adulterate the gospel, by substituting plausible speculations, or moral lectures in its stead; by narrowing and confining it within the limits of a nice system, which prevents the preacher from freely inviting sinners to come unto Christ; by representing the preparation of heart requisite to a sincere acceptance of free salvation as a *legal condition* of being received by him; or by condemning all diligence, repentance, and tenderness of conscience, as interfering with an evangelical frame of spirit. By these, and various other misapprehensions, the passage over the Slough is made worse, and they occasion manifold discouragements to awakened sinners, even to this day. For, as the *promises,* strictly speaking, belong only to believers; if *invitations* and exhortations be not freely given to sinners in general, a kind of gulf will be formed, over which no way can be seen: except as men take it for granted, *without any kind of evidence*, that they are true believers, which opens the door to manifold delusions and enthusiastic pretensions. But if all be invited, and encouraged to ask that they may receive; the awakened sinner will be animated to hope in God's mercy and use the means of grace, and thus giving diligence to make his calling and election sure, he will be enabled to rise superior to the discouragements, by which others are retarded. Laborers enough indeed are ready to lend their assistance, in mending the road across this Slough; but let them take care that they use none but scriptural materials, or they will make bad worse.

But that we shall meet with what fears and snares, with what troubles and afflictions, they can possibly assault us with that hate us.—Some persons are discouraged by recollecting past sins, and imagining them too heinous to be forgiven; while others disquiet themselves by the apprehension, that they have never been truly humbled and converted. Indeed all the varieties in the experience of those, who upon the whole are walking in the same path, can never be enumerated; and some of them are not only unreasonable, but unaccountable, through the weakness of the human mind, the abiding effects of peculiar impressions, the remains of unbelief, and the artifices of Satan.

Then said the keeper of the gate, Who is there? So the dog left off to bark, and he opened unto them.—The greater fervency new converts manifest in prayer for themselves and each other, the more violent opposition will they experience from the powers of darkness. Many have felt such terrors whenever they attempted to pray, that they have for a time been induced wholly to desist: and doubtless numbers, whose convictions were superficial, have thus been finally driven back to their former course of ungodliness. But when the fear of God, and a real belief of his word possess the heart, such disturbances cannot long prevent earnest cries for mercy; nay, they will eventually render them more fervent and importunate than ever.

Showed them by what deed they were saved; and told them withal, that that sight they would have again as they went along in the way, to their comfort.—*Pardon by word* seems to denote the general discovery of free salvation by Jesus Christ to all that believe; which, being depended on by the humble sinner, is sealed by transient comforts and lively affections. *Pardon by deed* may relate to the *manner*, in which the blessing was purchased by the Savior; and when this is clearly understood, the believer attains to stable peace and hope. This coincides with the explanation already given of the *Gate*, the *Cross*, and the *Sepulchre;* and it will be further confirmed in the sequel. The 'pardon by deed' must be waited for; yet the Pilgrims obtained a distant glimpse of the deed by which they were saved; for some general apprehensions of redemption by the cross of Christ are commonly connected with the believer's first comforts, though the nature and glory of it be more fully perceived as he proceeds.

And afraid I was to knock any more: but, when I looked up, to what was written over the gate, I took courage.—The express words of scriptural invitations, exhortations and promises prove more effectual to encourage those who are ready to give up their hopes, than all the consolatory topics that can possibly be substituted in their place. It is, therefore, much to be lamented, that pious men, by adhering to a systematical exactness of expression, should clog their addresses to sinners with exceptions and limitations, which the Spirit of God did not see good to insert. They will not say that the omission was an oversight in the inspired writers; or admit the thought for a moment, that they can improve on their plan; why then cannot they be satisfied to 'speak according to the oracles of God,' without affecting a more entire consistency? Great mischief has thus been done by very different descriptions of men, who undesignedly concur in giving Satan an occasion of suggesting to the trembling inquirer, that perhaps he may persevere in asking, seeking, and knocking, with the greatest earnestness and importunity, and yet finally be a cast-away!

I believe what you did pleased him well, for he showed no sign to the contrary.—When the sinner prays under the urgent fear of perishing, he is excited to peculiar fervency of spirit: and the more fervent our prayers are, the better are they approved by the Lord, how much soever men may object to the manner or expressions of them.

But I marvel in my heart why he keeps such a dog: had I known that afore, I should not have had heart enough to have ventured myself in this manner.—Could soldiers, when they enlist, foresee all the dangers and hardships to be encountered; or could mariners, when about to set sail, be fully aware of all the difficulties of the voyage; their reluctancy or discouragement would be increased by the prospect. But, when they have engaged, they find it impossible to recede; and thus they press forward through one labor and peril after another, till the campaign or voyage be accomplished. Thus it is with the Christian: but *they* strive for corruptible things, which they may never live to obtain; while *he* seeks for an incorruptible crown of glory, of which no event can deprive him. If *he* knew all from the first, it would be his only wisdom to venture: whereas the case with *them* is often widely different.

Their mother did also chide them for so doing, but still the boys went on.—The terrifying suggestions of Satan give believers much present uneasiness; yet they often do them great good, and seldom eventually hurt them: but the allurements of those worldly objects which he throws in their way, are far more dangerous and pernicious. Many of these, for which the aged have no longer any relish, are very attractive to *young persons:* but, all those parents or aged persons, who love the souls of their children and young friends, instead of conniving at them in their self-indulgence, from a notion, that allowance must be made for youth, should employ all their influence and authority to restrain them from those vain pleasures which 'war against the soul,' and are most dangerous when least suspected. This fruit may be found in the Pilgrim's path; but it grows in Beelzebub's garden, and should be shunned as poison. Many diversions and pursuits, both in high and low life, are of this nature, though often pleaded for as *innocent*, by some persons who ought to know better.

So all things work for good, and tend to make you more wary.—Satan designs, by every means, to take off awakened sinners from the great concern of eternal salvation; and he makes use of ungodly men for that purpose, among his manifold devices against the female sex. These are *very ill-favored* to the gracious mind; however alluring their persons, circumstances, or proposals may be to the carnal eye. As such vile seducers are too often successful, they are emboldened to attempt even those who profess to be religious: nor are they always repulsed by them; for many, of whom favorable hopes were once entertained, have thus awfully 'been again entangled and overcome, so that their last state has been worse than the first.' But when such proposals are repulsed with decided abhorrence, and earnest prayers, the Lord will give deliverance and victory. The faithful admonitions and warnings of a stated pastor are especially intended by the *Conductor*. The *Reliever* seems to represent the occasional direction and good counsel of some able minister; for he speaks of Christ, as his Lord, and must therefore be considered as one of the servants by whom help is sent to the distressed.

PART II · CHAPTER III

THE INTERPRETER'S HOUSE

Straws, and sticks, and dust, with most, are the great things now looked after.—The emblematical instruction at the Interpreter's house, in the former part, was so important and comprehensive, that no other selection equally interesting could be expected: some valuable hints, however, are here adduced. The first emblem is very plain; and so apposite, that it is wonderful any person should read it without lifting up a prayer to the Lord, and saying, 'O! deliver me from this muck-rake.' Yet, alas, it is to be feared, such prayers are still little used even by professors of the gospel; at least they are contradicted by the habitual conduct of numbers among them; and this may properly lead us to weep over others, and tremble for ourselves.

Yet she had taken hold with her hands, and, as I see, dwelleth in the best room in the house.—God has made nothing in vain.—The instruction grounded on accommodation of Scripture, though solid and important, is not so convincing to the understanding, as that which results from the obvious meaning of the words; though many persons are for the time more excited to attention, by a lively exercise of the imagination, and the surprise of unexpected inferences. This method, however, should be used with great caution by the friends of truth; for it is a most formidable engine in the hands of those, who endeavor to pervert or oppose it. The author did not, however, mean by the emblem of the spider, that the sinner might confidently assure himself of salvation, by the blood of Christ, while he continued full of the poison of sin, without experiencing or evidencing any change; but only, that no consciousness of inward pollution, or actual guilt, should discourage any one from *applying* to Christ, and *'fleeing* for refuge to lay hold on the hope set before him,' that thus he may be delivered from condemnation, and cleansed from pollution, and so made meet for those blessed mansions, into which no unclean thing can find admission.

I choose, my darlings, to lead you into the room where such things are, because you are women, and they are easy for you.—Our Lord hath, in immense condescension, employed this emblem, to represent his tender love to his people, for whom he bare the storm of wrath himself, that they might be safe and happy under 'the shadow of his wings.' (Matthew 23:37.) The *common call* signifies the general invitations of the gospel, which should be addressed without restriction, to all men that come under the sound of it; 'as many as ye find, bid to the marriage.' The *special call* denotes those influences of the Spirit, by which the heart is sweetly made willing to embrace the invitation, and apply for the blessing, in the use of the appointed means, by which sinners actually experience the accomplishment of the promises, as their circumstances require. The *brooding note* was intended to represent that communion with God, and those consolations of the Holy Spirit, which the Scriptures encourage us to expect, and by which the believer is trained up for eternal felicity: whilst the *out-cry* refers to the warnings and cautions, by which believers are excited to vigilance, circumspection, and self-examination, and to beware of all deceivers and delusions.

Where the gardener hath set them, there they stand, and quarrel not one with another.—We ought not to be contented, (so to speak,) with a situation among the useless and noxious weeds of the desert: but if we be planted among the ornamental and fragrant flowers of the Lord's garden, we may deem ourselves sufficiently distinguished and honored. We should, therefore, watch against envy and ambition, contempt of our brethren, and contention. We ought to be satisfied in our place, doing 'nothing through strife or vain-glory,' or 'with murmurings and disputings:' but endeavoring, in the meekness of wisdom, to diffuse a heavenly fragrance around us, and 'to adorn the doctrine of God our Savior in all things.'

Fruit, you see, is that thing you look for, and for want of that you condemn it to the fire, and to be trodden under foot of men: beware that in this you condemn not your yourselves.—The labor and expense of the husbandman are not repaid by the straw or the chaff, but by the corn. The humiliation and sufferings of Christ, the publication of the gospel, the promises and instituted ordinances, and the labor of ministers, were not intended merely to bring men to profess certain doctrines, and observe certain forms; or even to produce convictions, affections, or comforts, in any order or degree whatsoever; but to render men fruitful in good works, by the influences of the Spirit of Christ, and through his sanctifying truth: and all profession will terminate in everlasting contempt and misery, which is not productive of this good fruit, whatever men may pretend, or however they may deceive themselves and one another.

One leak will sink a ship: and one sin will destroy a sinner.—By repentance and faith in Christ, the leaks that sin hath made, are, as it were, stopped; but one sin, habitually committed with allowance, proves a man's profession hypocritical, however plausible it may be in all other respects; as one leak unstopped will assuredly at length sink the ship.

We seldom sit down to meat, but we eat and leave: so there is in Jesus Christ more merit and righteousness than the whole world has need of.—This observation is grounded on the good old distinction, that the merit of Christ's obedience unto death is *sufficient for all*, though only *effectual to some;* namely, in one view of the subject, *to the elect:* in another, *to all who by faith apply for an interest in it.* This makes way for general invitations, and shows it to be every one's duty to repent and believe the gospel; as nothing but pride, the carnal mind, and enmity to God and religion, influence men to neglect so great salvation; and, when the regenerating power of the Holy Spirit accompanies the word, sinners are made willing to accept the proffered mercy, and encouraged by the general invitations, which before they sinfully slighted.

Interpreter: Thy setting out is good, for thou hast given credit to the truth.—This is a most simple definition of faith: it is 'the belief of the truth,' as the sure testimony of God, relative to our most important concerns. When we thus credit those truths that teach us the peril of our situation as justly condemned sinners, we are moved with fear, and humbled in repentance; and when we thus believe the report of a refuge provided for us, our hopes are excited. Those truths that relate to inestimable blessings attainable by us, when really credited, kindle our fervent desires; while such as show us the glory, excellency and mercy of God our Savior, and our obligations to his redeeming grace, work by love, gratitude, and every fervent affection. This living faith influences a man's judgment, choice, and conduct; and especially induces him to receive Jesus Christ for all the purposes of salvation, and to yield himself to his service, as constrained by love of him and zeal for his glory. We need no other ground for this faith, than the authenticated word of God. This may be brought to our recollection by means of distress or danger, or even in a dream, or with some very strong impression on the mind: yet true faith rests only on the word of God, *according to its meaning as it stands in the Bible;* and not in the manner in which it occurs to the thoughts, or according to any *new sense put upon it in a dream, or by an impression;* as this would be a *new revelation.* For if the words, 'Thy sins are forgiven thee,' should be impressed on *my mind*, they would contain a declaration no where made in Scripture *concerning me;* consequently the belief of them on this ground would be a faith not warranted by the word of God. Now as we have no reason to expect such new revelations, and as Satan can counterfeit any of these impressions, we must consider every thing of this kind as opening a door to enthusiasm, and the most dangerous delusions; though many, who rest their confidence on them, have also scriptural evidence of their acceptance, which they overlook. On the other hand, should the following words be powerfully impressed on my mind, 'Him that cometh to me I will in no wise cast out,' or, 'He that confesseth and forsaketh his sin shall find mercy;' I may deduce encouragement from the words, according to the genuine meaning of them as they stand in Scripture, without any dread of delusion, or any pretence to new revelations; provided I be conscious, that I do come to Christ, and confess my sins with the sincere purpose of forsaking them. But there are so many dangers in this matter, that the more evidently our faith and hope are grounded wholly on the plain testimony of God, and confirmed by our subsequent experience and conduct; the safer will our course be, and the less occasion will be given to the objections of our despisers.

It also added to their gravity, and made their countenances more like those of angels.—The author calls this 'The Bath of sanctification,' in a marginal note: whence we may infer, that he especially meant to intimate, that believers should constantly seek fresh supplies of grace from the Holy Spirit, to purify their hearts from the renewed defilement of sin, which their intercourse with the world will continually occasion; and to revive and invigorate those holy affections, which in the same manner are apt to grow languid. Yet he did not intend to exclude their habitual reliance on the blood of Christ for pardon and acceptance; for in both respects we need daily washing. The sanctification of the Spirit unto obedience warrants the true Christian's 'peace and joy in believing;' it gives him beauty in the sight of his brethren; it strengthens him for every conflict, and service; and the image of Christ, discernible in the spirit and conduct, *seals* him as a child of God and an heir of glory: while the inward consciousness of living by faith in the Son of God for all the blessings of salvation, and experiencing all filial affections towards God as his reconciled Father inspires him with humble joy and confidence.

The children also stood amazed, to see into what fashion they were brought.—The Pilgrims are supposed to have been justified on their admission at the Gate; the Interpreter is the emblem of the Holy Spirit; and the raiment here mentioned rendered those who were adorned with it comely in the eyes of their companions. We cannot, therefore, with propriety explain it to signify the righteousness of Christ imputed to the believer, but the renewal of the soul to holiness; for this alone in its effects is visible to the eyes of men. They, who have put on this raiment, are also 'clothed with humility:' so that they readily perceive the excellencies of other believers, but cannot discern their own, except when they look in the glass of God's word. At the same time they become very observant of their own defects, and severe in animadverting on them, but proportionably candid to their brethren: and thus they learn the hard lesson of 'esteeming others better than themselves.'

And take these my daughters, said he; conduct them to the house called Beautiful, at which place they will rest next.—The stated pastoral care of a vigilant minister, who is strong in faith, and courageous in the cause of God, is represented by the conductor of the Pilgrims. We shall have repeated opportunities of showing, how desirous the author was to recommend this advantage to his readers, to excite them to be thankful for it, and to avail themselves of it when graciously afforded them.

PART II · CHAPTER IV

THE CROSS AND THE CONSEQUENCES

Thus has he ransomed you from your transgressions by blood, and covered your polluted and deformed souls with righteousness; for the sake of which, God passeth by you, and will not hurt you when he comes to judge the world.—This discourse, on 'Pardon by the deed done,' confirms the interpretation that hath been given of the Cross, and of Christian's deliverance from his burden. The doctrine is, however, here stated in a manner to which some may object, and indeed it is needlessly systematical and rather obscure. By 'the righteousness of Christ, as God,' his essential divine attributes of justice and holiness must be intended. 'His righteousness, as Man,' denotes his human nature as free from all the defilements of sin. 'The righteousness of his person, as he hath the two natures joined in one,' can only mean the perfection of his mysterious person in all respects: and his capacity of acting as our Surety, by doing and suffering in our nature all that was requisite, while his divine nature stamped an infinite value on his obedience unto death. The eternal Word, the only begotten Son of God, was under no obligation to assume our nature; and when he had seen good to assume it, he was not bound to live a number of years here on earth, obedient to the law, both in its ceremonial and moral requirements, amidst hardships, sufferings, and temptations of every kind; except, as he had undertaken to be our Surety. In this sense he himself had no need of that righteousness which he finished for our justification. And assuredly he was under no obligation, as a perfectly holy man, to suffer any thing, much less to submit to the violent, torturing, and ignominious death upon the cross. That part of his obedience, which consisted in enduring agony and pain in body and soul, was only needful, as he bare our sins, and gave himself a sacrifice to God for us. Indeed, his righteousness is not the less his own, by being imputed to us: for believers are considered as one with him, and thus 'made the righteousness of God in him,' and we are justified in virtue of this union. He was able by his temporal sufferings and death to pay our debts, and ransom our inheritance; thus delivering us from eternal misery which else had been inevitable, and bringing us to eternal life which had otherwise been unattainable; and the law of love, to which as a man he became subject, required him to do this; for if we 'loved our neighbor as ourselves,' we should be willing to submit to any inferior loss, hardship, or suffering, to rescue an enemy or stranger from a greater and more durable misery, which he has no other way of escaping; or to secure to him a more valuable and permanent advantage which can no otherwise be obtained.

Surely, surely their hearts would be affected; nor could the fear of the one, nor the powerful lusts of the other, prevail with them to go home again, and refuse to become good pilgrims.—When believers, 'in the warmth of their affections,' feel the humbling, melting, endearing, and sanctifying effects of contemplating the glory of the Cross, and the love of Christ in dying for sinners; and consider themselves as the special objects of that inexpressible compassion and kindness; they are apt to conclude that the belief of the propositions, that *Christ loves them and died for them, and that God is reconciled to them,* produces the change by its own influence: and would affect the most carnal hearts in the same manner, could men be persuaded to believe it. For they vainly imagine that apprehensions of the severity of divine justice, and the dread of vengeance, are the sources of the enmity which sinners manifest against God. Hence very lively and affectionate Christians have frequently been prone to sanction the unscriptural tenet, that the justifying act of faith consists in *assuredly believing that Christ died for me in particular, and that God loves me;* and to consider this *appropriation* as preceding repentance, and every other gracious disposition; and as in some sense the cause of regeneration, winning the heart to love God, and to rejoice in him, and in obeying his commandments. From this doctrine others have inferred, that if all men, and even devils too, believed the love of God to them, and his purpose at length to make them happy, they would be won over from rebellion against him, which they persist in from a mistaken idea that he is their implacable enemy: and they make this one main argument, in support of the salutary tendency of the final restitution scheme. But all these opinions arise from a false and flattering estimate of human nature; for the carnal mind hates the scriptural character of God and the glory displayed in the cross, even more than that which shines forth in the fiery law. Indeed if we take away the *offensive part* of the gospel, the honor it puts upon the law and its awful sanctions, and the exhibition it makes of the divine justice and holiness, it will give the proud carnal heart but little umbrage: if we admit that men's aversion to God and religion arises from misapprehension, and not from desperate wickedness, many will endure the doctrine. A reconciliation, in which God assures the sinner that he has forgiven him, even before he has repented of his sins, will suit man's pride; and if he has been previously frighted, a great flow of affections may follow: but the event will prove, that they differ essentially from spiritual love of God, gratitude, holy joy, and genuine humiliation, which arise from a true perception of the glorious perfections of God, the righteousness of his law and government, the real nature of redemption, and the odiousness and desert of sin. In short, all such schemes *render regeneration needless*, or substitute something else in its stead, which is effected by a *natural process*, and not by the *new-creating power of the Holy Spirit*. But, when this divine agent has communicated life to the soul, and a capacity is produced of perceiving and relishing spiritual excellency, the enmity against God receives a mortal wound: from that season, the more his real character and glory are known, the greater spiritual affection will be excited, and a proportionable transformation into the same holy image effected. Then the view of the cross, as the grand display of all the harmonious perfections of the Godhead, softens, humbles, and meliorates the heart: while the persuasion of an interest in these blessings, and an admiring sense of having received such inconceivable favors from this glorious and holy Lord God, will still further elevate the soul above all low pursuits, and constrain it to the most unreserved and self-denying obedience.

But, while the heart remains unregenerate, the glory of God and the gospel will either be misunderstood, or hated in proportion as it is discovered. Such views and affections therefore as have been described, spring from special grace; and are not produced by the natural efficacy of any sentiments, but by the immediate influences of the Holy Spirit; so that even true believers, though they habitually are persuaded of their interest in Christ, and the love of God to them, are only at times thus filled with holy affections; nor will the same contemplations constantly excite similar exercises; but they often bestow much pains to get their minds affected by them in vain; while at other times a single glance of thought fills them with the most fervent emotions of holy love and joy.

They would call the bread of God, husks; the comforts of his children, fancies; the travail and labor of pilgrims, things to no purpose.—The dreadful falls and awful deaths of some professors are often made notorious, for a warning to others; and to put them upon their guard against superficial, slothful, and presumptuous men, who draw aside many from the holy ways of God. The names of the persons thus deluded show the reasons why men listen to deceivers; for these are only the *occasions* of their turning aside, the *cause* lies in the concealed lusts of their own hearts. The transition is very easy from orthodox notions and profession without experience, to false and loose sentiments, and then to open ungodliness.

These lines are here inserted under a plate:—

> Behold here how the slothful are a sign
> Hung up 'cause holy ways they did decline:
> See here too, how the child doth play the man,
> And weak grow strong, when Great-heart leads the van.

They took it up, and put it into an earthen pot, and so let it stand till the dirt was gone to the bottom, and then they drank thereof.—This passage shows, that the *preaching of the gospel* was especially intended by *the spring*, in the former part of the work. Since that had been published, the author had witnessed a departure from the simplicity of the gospel, as it has been before observed. This might be done unadvisedly in those immediately concerned; but it originated from the devices of evil men, and the subtlety of Satan. They, however, who honestly and carefully aimed to distinguish between the precious and the vile, might separate the corrupt part from the truths of God, and from the latter derive comfort and establishment.

You shall see that these ways are made cautionary enough, not only by these posts, and ditch, and chain, but also by being hedged up; yet they will choose to go there.—The express declarations, commandments and warnings of Scripture; and the heart-searching doctrines and distinguishing application of faithful ministers, sufficiently hedge up all those by-ways, into which professors are tempted to turn aside: but carnal self-love, and desire of ease to the flesh, (which always opposes its own crucifixion,) induce numbers to break through all obstacles, and to risk their eternal interests, rather than deny themselves, and endure hardship in the way to heaven. Nor will teachers be wanting to flatter them with the hope of being saved by *notionally* believing certain doctrines, while they *practically* treat the whole word of God as a lie!

"What shall be given unto thee, or what shall be done unto thee, thou false tongue? Sharp arrows of the mighty, with coals of juniper."—The word David signifies *Beloved*. We should be very cautious not to speak any thing, which may discourage such as seem disposed to a religious life; lest we should be found to have abetted that enemy, who spares no pains to seduce them back again into the world. Even the unbelieving fears and complaints of weak and tempted Christians should be repressed before persons of this description: how great then will be the guilt of those who stifle their own convictions, and act contrary to their conscience, from fear of reproach or persecution, and then employ themselves in dissuading others from serving God!

The boys also looked as if they would die; but they all got by without further hurt.—It is not very easy to determine the precise idea of the author, in each of the Giants, who assault the Pilgrims, and are slain by the conductor and his assistants. Some have supposed that *unbelief* is here meant: but Grim, or Bloody-man, seems not to be apposite names for this inward foe; nor can it be conceived that *unbelief* should more violently assault those, who are under the care of a valiant conductor, than it had done the solitary Pilgrims. I apprehend, therefore, that this Giant was intended for the emblem of certain active men, who busied themselves in framing and executing persecuting statutes; which was done at the time when this was written more violently than it had been before. Thus the temptation to fear man, which at all times assaults the believer, when required to make an open profession of his faith, was exceedingly increased: and, as heavy fines and severe penalties, in accession to reproach and contempt, deterred men from joining themselves in communion with dissenting churches, that way was almost unoccupied, and the travellers went through by-paths, according to the author's sentiments on the subject. But the preaching of the gospel, by which the ministers of Christ wielded the sword of the Spirit, overcame this enemy: for the example and exhortations of such courageous combatants animated even weak believers to overcome their fears, and to act according to their consciences, leaving the event to God. This seems to have been the author's meaning; and perhaps he also intended to encourage his brethren boldly to persevere in resisting such persecuting statutes, confidently expecting that they should prevail for the repeal of them; by which, as by the death of the Giant, the Pilgrims might be freed from additional terror, in acting consistently with their avowed principles.

PART II · CHAPTER V

THE PALACE BEAUTIFUL

For when he bid me come thus far with you, then you should have begged me of him to have gone quite through with you, and he would have granted your request.—We are repeatedly reminded, with great propriety, that we ought to be very particular and explicit in our prayers, especially in every thing pertaining to our spiritual advantage. The removal of faithful ministers, or the fear of losing them, may often remind Christians that 'here they have failed:' they have not sufficiently valued and prayed for them; or, making sure of their continuance, from apparent probabilities, they have not made that the subject of their peculiar requests, and therefore are rebuked by the loss of them.

Welcome, ye vessels of the grace of God, welcome unto us your friends.—'Angels rejoice over one sinner that repenteth;' and all, who truly love the Lord, will gladly welcome such as appear to be true believers, into their most endeared fellowship: yet there are certain individuals, who, being related to those that have greatly interested their hearts, or having long been remembered in their prayers, are welcomed with singular joy and satisfaction, and whose professed faith animates them in a peculiar manner.

They had prepared for them a lamb, with the accustomed sauce belonging thereto.—The passover was a prefiguration of the sufferings of Christ, and the believer's acceptance of him; of his professed reliance on the atoning sacrifice, preservation from wrath, and the deliverance from the bondage of Satan, to set out on his heavenly pilgrimage. And the Lord's supper is a commemorative ordinance of a similar import; representing the body of Christ broken for our sins, and his blood shed for us; the application of these blessings to our souls by faith, the profession of this faith and of love to him and his people, influencing us to devoted, self-denying obedience: and the effects which follow from thus 'feeding on Christ in our hearts by faith with thanksgiving,' in strengthening us for every conflict and service to which we are called. 'The unleavened bread of sincerity and truth,' and 'the bitter herbs' of godly sorrow, deep repentance, mortification of sin, and bearing the cross, accompany the spiritual feast; and even render it more relishing to the true believer, as endearing to him Christ and his salvation.

Mercy: And you as little thought of lying in his bed, and in his chamber to rest as you do now.—A marginal note here says, 'Christ's bosom is for all Pilgrims.' The sweet peace arising from calm confidence in the Savior, the consolations of his Spirit, submission to his will, and the cheerful obedience of fervent love, give rest to the soul, as if we were reclining on his bosom with the beloved disciple. (See PART I - Christian's bed-chamber.)

That it was a good dream; and that, as you have begun to find the first part true, so you shall find the second at last.—They who feel and lament the hardness of their hearts, and earnestly pray that they may be humbled, softened, and filled with the love of Christ, may be assured that their sorrow shall be turned into joy: though they must expect to be ridiculed by such as know not their own hearts. The assurance, that the dream should be accomplished, is grounded on the effects produced upon Mercy's heart; and there is no danger of delusion, when so scriptural an encouragement is inferred even from a dream.

James: By his grace.—Grace, in this connection, signifies unmerited mercy or favor, from which all the blessings of salvation flow. The Father freely gave his Son to be our Redeemer, and now freely communicates his Spirit, through the merits and mediation of the Son, to be our Sanctifier; and thus, with Christ, he *freely* gives all things to those, who are enabled truly to believe in him. The important, but much neglected duty of catechizing children is here very properly inculcated; without attention to which, the minister's labors, both in public preaching and private instruction, will be understood in a very imperfect degree; and any revival of religion that takes place, will probably die with the generation to which it is vouchsafed.

Joseph: Those that accept of his salvation.—The young pupil is not here taught to answer *systematically*, 'All the elect:' but *practically*, 'Those that accept of his salvation.' This is perfectly consistent with the other; but it is suited to instruct and encourage the learner who would be perplexed, stumbled, or misled by the other view of the same truth. Thus our Lord observed to his disciples, 'I have many things to say unto you, but ye cannot bear them now;' and Paul fed the Corinthians, 'with milk, and not with meat; for they were not able to bear it.' How beneficial would a portion of the same heavenly wisdom prove to the modern friends of evangelical truth! And how absurd is it to teach the hardest lessons to the youngest scholars in the school of Christ!

Prudence: What do you do when you meet with places therein that you do not understand?—We ought not to think ourselves capable of comprehending all the mysteries of revelation, or informed of all that can be known concerning them: yet we should not make our incapacity a reason for neglecting those parts of Scripture, which we do not at present understand: but, uniting humble diligence with fervent prayers, we should wait for further light and knowledge, in all things conducive to our good. There may be many parts of Scripture, which would not be useful to *us*, if we could understand them; though they have been, are, or will be useful to others; and our inability to discover the meaning of these passages may teach us humility, and submission to the decisions of our infallible Instructor.

I will warrant her a good housewife, quoth he to himself.—Designing men will often assume an appearance of religion, in order to insinuate themselves into the affections of such pious young women, as are on some accounts agreeable to them; and thus many are drawn into a most dangerous snare. This incident therefore is very properly introduced, and is replete with instruction. At the same time an important intimation is given, concerning the manner in which those, who are not taken up with the care of a family, may profitably employ their time, adorn the gospel, and be useful in the church and the community. It is much better to imitate Dorcas, who 'through faith obtained a good report,' in making garments for the poor, than to waste time and money in frivolous amusements, or needless decorations; or even in the more elegant and fashionable accomplishments.

Mercy and he are of tempers so different, that I believe they will never come together.—Young people ought not wholly to follow their own judgments in this most important concern, on which the comfort and usefulness of their whole future lives in a great measure depend: and yet it is equally dangerous to advise with improper counsellors. The names of the maidens of the house, show what kind of persons should be consulted: and, when such friends are of opinion that there is danger of a *clog,* instead of a *helper,* in the way to heaven, all who love their own souls, will speedily determine to reject the proposal, however agreeable in all other respects. The apostolical rule, 'Only in the Lord,' is absolute. The most upright and cautious may indeed be deceived; but they, who neglect to ask, or refuse to take counsel, will be sure to smart for their folly, if they be indeed the children of God. An unbelieving partner must be a continual source of anxiety and uneasiness; a thorn in the side; and an hindrance to all family religion, and the pious education of children, who generally adhere to the maxims and practices of the ungodly party. Nothing tends more than such marriages, to induce a declining state of religion; or indeed more plainly shows that it is already in a very unprosperous state. But, when Christians plainly avow their principles, purposes, and rules of conduct, they may commonly detect and shake off such selfish pretenders: while the attempts made to injure their characters, will do them no material detriment, and will render them the more thankful for having escaped the snare.

Then Christiana began to cry; and she said, O naughty boy! and O careless mother! what shall I do for my son?—Sin, heedlessly or wilfully committed, after the Lord has spoken peace to our souls, often produces great distress long afterward; and sometimes darkness and discouragement oppress the mind, when the special cause of them is not immediately recollected: for we have grieved the Holy Spirit and he withholds his consolations. In this case we should adopt the prayer of Job, 'Do not condemn me; show me wherefore thou contendest with me:' and this inquiry will often be answered by the discourse of skilful ministers, and the faithful admonitions of our fellow Christians. When hopeful professors are greatly cast down, it is not wise to administer cordials to them immediately: but to propose such questions as may lead to a discovery of the concealed cause of their distress. Thus it will often be found, that they have been tampering with forbidden fruit; which discovery may tend to their humiliation, and produce a similar effect on those who have neglected their duty, by suffering others to sin without warning or reproof.

It caused him to purge, it caused him to sleep, and to rest quietly; it put him into a fine heat and breathing sweat, and it quite rid him of his gripes.—To support the allegory, the author gives the Physician's prescription in Latin; but he adds in the margin, with admirable modesty, *The Latin I borrow.* 'Without the shedding of blood, there is no remission of sins,' or true peace of conscience; 'the blood of bulls and goats cannot take away sin:' nothing, therefore, can bring health and cure, in this case, but the *'body and blood of Christ,'* as broken and shed for our sins. These blessings are made ours by faith exercised on the promises of God; the sanctifying grace of the Holy Spirit, which seasons our words and actions as with salt, always connects with living faith; and godly sorrow, working genuine repentance, is renewed every time we look to the Savior, whom we have pierced by our recent offences, and of whom we again seek forgiveness. The natural pride, stoutness, and unbelief of our hearts, render us very reluctant to this humiliating method of recovering peace and spiritual strength; and this often prolongs our distress: yet nothing yields more unalloyed comfort, than thus abasing ourselves before God, and relying on his mercy through the atonement and mediation of his beloved Son.

But, good Christiana, thou must give these pills no other way but as I have prescribed; for if you do, they will do no good.—This hint should be carefully noted. Numbers abuse the doctrine of free salvation, by the merit and redemption of Christ, and presume on forgiveness, when they are destitute of genuine repentance, and give no evidence of sanctification. But this most efficacious medicine in that case will 'do no good;' or rather the perverse abuse of it will increase their guilt, and tend to harden their hearts in sin.

Mr. Interpreter; who, when it was come, and he had seen the contents of the petition, said to the messenger, Go tell them that I will send him.—This may be applied to the case of persons who are unavoidably removed from those places, where they first made an open profession of the faith. The vigilant pastor, who can no longer watch for their souls, will earnestly recommend them to the care of some other minister, and join with them in prayer, that the same faithful services, or better, may be rendered them by other servants of their common Lord.

So they opened the matter to her, and she held up her hands and wondered.—The nature of the first transgression; the ambiguous insinuations by which the tempter seduced Eve, and by her, Adam; the motives from which they ate the forbidden fruit; and the dreadful disappointment that followed; with all the aggravations and consequences of that most prolific offence, which contained in it, as in miniature and embryo, all future sins, are very instructive and affecting to the pious mind. For the enemy still proceeds against us, according to the same general plan; suggesting hard thoughts of God, doubts about the restrictions and threatenings of his word, proud desires of independence or useless knowledge, hankerings after forbidden indulgence, and hopes of enjoying the pleasures of sin, without feeling the punishment denounced against transgressors.

So they turned again, and stood feeding their eyes with this so pleasant a prospect.—Christ, in his person and offices, is the *medium* of communication between heaven and earth, between God and man: by him sinners come to God with acceptance, and God dwells with them and is glorified; through him they present their worship and services, and receive supplies of all heavenly blessings; and for his sake angels delight in 'ministering to the heirs of salvation,' as instruments of his providential care over them and all their concerns. This was represented or typified by Jacob's *ladder*.

That you may lay hold of that within the veil, and stand steadfast in case you should meet with turbulent weather; so they were glad thereof.—The hope of glory, or of the fulfilment of all God's promises to our souls, is the golden *Anchor,* by which we must be kept steadfast in the faith, and encouraged to abide in our proper station, amidst the storms of temptation, affliction, and persecution. This it will certainly effect; provided it be genuine and living, grounded on the word of God, springing from faith in his Son, warranted by the experience of his grace, and accompanied by prevailing desires of a holy felicity, in the presence, favor, and service of the Lord.

PART II · CHAPTER VI

THE VALLEY OF HUMILIATION

Let Him grant that dwelleth above, that we fare not worse, when we come to be tried, than he.—As the author here evidently alluded to some particulars in his own experience, a more explicit account of these slips would have been very interesting and instructive; but as it is, we can only conjecture his meaning. He probably referred to some erroneous conclusions which he had formed, concerning the measure of the Lord's dealings with his people, and the nature of their situation in this world. Having obtained peace and comfort, and enjoyed sweet satisfaction in communion with his brethren, he expected the continuance of this happy frame, and considered it as the evidence of his acceptance: so that afflictions and humiliating discoveries of the evils of his heart, by interrupting his comforts, induced him to conclude that his past experience was a delusion, and that God was become his enemy; and this unscriptural way of judging concerning his state seems to have made way for the dark temptations that followed. Were it not for such mistakes, humiliating dispensations and experiences would not have any necessary connection with terror; and they would give less occasion to temptations than prosperity and comfort do: while a lowly condition is exempted from the numberless snares, incumbrances, and anxieties of a more exalted station: and humility is the parent of patience, meekness, contentment, thankfulness, and every holy disposition that can enrich and adorn the soul. A far greater proportion of believers are found in inferior circumstances, than among the wealthy; and they who are kept low commonly thrive the best, and are most simple and diligent. Without poverty of spirit, we cannot possess 'the unsearchable riches of Christ:' and more promises are made to the humble, than to any other character whatsoever.

That they might be troubled no more with either hills or mountains to go over: but the way is the way, and there is an end.—The consolations of humble believers, even in their lowest abasement, when favored by the exhilarating and fertilizing beams of the Sun of Righteousness, are represented under this emblem. The *lilies* are the harmless and holy disciples of Christ, who adorn a poor and obscure condition of life; and who are an ornament to religion, being 'clothed with humility.' Many grow rich in faith and good works in retirement and obscurity; and become averse, even at the call of duty, to emerge from it, lest any advancement should lead them into temptation, stir up their pride, or expose them to envy and contention.

This boy lives a merrier life, and wears more of that herb called heart's-ease in his bosom, than he that is clad in silk and velvet. But we will proceed in our discourse.—Perhaps the *Shepherd's boy* may refer to the obscure but quiet station of some pastors over small congregations, who live almost unknown to their brethren, but are in a measure useful, and very comfortable.

He has left a yearly revenue to be faithfully paid them at certain seasons for their maintenance by the way, and for their further encouragement to go on in their pilgrimage.—Our Lord chose retirement, poverty, and an obscure station, as the rest and delight of his own mind; as remote from bustle and contention, and favorable to contemplation and devotion: so that his appearance in a public character, and in crowded scenes, for the good of mankind and the glory of the Father, was a part of his self-denial, in which 'he pleased not himself.' Indeed there is a peculiar congeniality between a lowly mind, and a lowly condition: and as much violence is done to the inclinations of the humble, when they are rendered conspicuous and advanced to high stations, as to those of the haughty, when they are thrust down into obscurity and neglect. Other men seem to be *banished* into this Valley; but the poor in spirit love to walk in it: and, though some believers here struggle with distressing temptations, others in passing through it enjoy much communion with God.

For if at any time pilgrims meet with any brunt, it is when they forget what favors they have received, and how unworthy they are of them.—When consolations and privileges betray us into *forgetfulness* of our entire unworthiness of such special favors, humiliating dispensations commonly ensue; and these sometimes reciprocally excite murmurs and *forgetfulness* of past mercies. Thus Satan gains an opportunity of assaulting the soul with dreadful temptations: and, while at one moment hard thoughts of God, or doubts concerning the truth of his word, are suggested to our minds; at the next we may be affrighted by our own dreadful rebellion and ingratitude, prompted to condemn ourselves as hypocrites, and almost driven to despair.

Lo, yonder also stands a monument, on which is engraven this battle, and Christian's victory, to his fame throughout all ages.—We ought carefully to study the records left us of the temptations, conflicts, faith, patience, and victories of other believers: we should mark well, what wounds they received, and by what misconduct they were occasioned, that we may watch and pray lest we fall in like manner. We ought carefully to observe, how they successfully repelled the various assaults of the tempter, that we may learn to resist him, steadfast in the faith; and in general, their triumphs should animate us, to 'put on,' and keep on, 'the whole armor of God, that we may be enabled to withstand in the evil day.' On the other hand, such as have been rendered victorious should readily speak of their experiences *among those that fear* God, that they may be cautioned, instructed, and encouraged by their example.

But the guide also bid them be of good courage, and look well to their feet, lest haply, said he, you be taken in some snare.—The meaning of this valley has been stated in the notes on the first part of this work; and the interpretation there given is here confirmed. As it relates chiefly to the influence, which 'the Prince of the power of the air' possesses over the imagination; it must vary exceedingly, according to the constitution, animal spirits, health, education, and strength of mind or judgment, of different persons. They, who are *happily* incapable of understanding either the allegory or the explanation, should beware of despising or condemning such as have been thus harassed. And, on the other hand, these should take care not to consider such temptations as proofs of spiritual advancement: or to yield to them, as if they were essential to maturity of grace and experience; by which means Satan often attains dreadful advantages. It is most advisable for tempted persons to consult some able, judicious minister, or compassionate and established Christian, whose counsel and prayers may be singularly useful in this case; observing the assistance which Great-heart gave to the Pilgrims, in passing through the valley.

There is not such pleasant being here as at the gate, or at the Interpreter's, or at the house where we lay last.— Whatever attempts Satan may make to terrify the believer, resolute resistance by faith in Christ will drive him away: but if fear induces men to neglect the means of grace, he will renew his assaults on the imagination, whenever they attempt to pray, read the scripture, or attend on any duty; till for a time, or finally, they give up their religion. In this case, therefore, determined perseverance in opposition to every terrifying suggestion is our only safety. Yet sometimes temptations may be so multiplied and varied, that it may seem impossible to proceed any further; and the mind of the harassed believer is enveloped in confusion and dismay, as if an horrible pit were about to swallow him up, or the Prince of darkness to seize upon him. But the counsel of some experienced friend or minister, exciting confidence in the power, mercy, and faithfulness of God, and encouraging him to "pray without ceasing," will at length make way for his deliverance.

Why, if ever I get out here again, said the boy, I think I shall prize light and good way better than ever I did in all my life.—Should any one, by hearing the believer say, 'The sorrows of death compassed me, and the pains of hell gat hold upon me,' be tempted to avoid all religious duties, company, and reflections, lest he should experience similar terrors, let him well weigh this observation: 'It is not so bad to go through here, as to abide here always.' Nothing can be more absurd, than to neglect religion, lest the fear of hell should discompose a man's mind, when such neglect exposes him to the external endurance of it: whereas the short taste of distress, which may be experienced by the tempted believer, will make redemption more precious, and render peace, comfort, and heaven at last, doubly delightful!

But he was beloved of his God: also he had a good heart of his own, or else he could never have done it.—The discouragement of dark temptations is not so formidable, in the judgment of experienced Christians, as the snares connected with them: for, while numbers renounce their profession, to get rid of their disquietude; many are seduced into some false doctrine that may sanction negligence, and quiet their consciences by assenting to certain notions, without regarding the state of their hearts, or what passes in their experience; and others are led to spend all their time in company, or even to dissipate the gloom by engaging in worldly amusements, because retirement exposes them to these suggestions. In short, the enemy endeavors to terrify the professor, that he may drive him away from God, entangle him in heresy, or draw him into sin; in order to destroy his soul, or at least ruin his credit and prevent his usefulness. But circumspection and prayer constitute our best preservative; through which, they who *take heed* to their steps escape, while the *heedless* are taken and destroyed, for a warning to those that come after.

Until that I Great-heart arose, The pilgrims' guide to be; Until that I did him oppose, That was their enemy.— This giant came out of *the cave,* where Pope and Pagan had resided. He is therefore the emblem of those formal superstitious teachers, and those speculating moralists, who in protestant countries have too generally succeeded the Romish priests and the heathen philosophers, in keeping men ignorant of the way of salvation, and in spoiling by their sophistry such as seem to be seriously disposed. These persons often represent faithful ministers, who draw off their auditors, by preaching 'repentance towards God, and faith towards our Lord Jesus Christ,' as robbers and kidnappers: they terrify many, (especially when they have the power of enforcing penal statutes,) from professing or hearing the gospel, and acting according to their consciences; and they put the faith of God's servants to a severe trial. Yet perseverance, patience, and prayer, will obtain the victory; and they that are strong will be instrumental in animating the feeble to go on their way rejoicing and praising God. But though these enemies may be baffled, disabled, or apparently slain, it will appear that they have left a posterity on earth, to revile, injure, and oppose the spiritual worshippers of God in every generation. The club with which the giant was armed, may mean the secular arm or power by which opposers of the gospel are generally desirous of enforcing their arguments and persuasions. 'We have a law, and by our law he ought to die;' this decision, like a heavy club, seems capable of bearing all down before it: nor can any withstand its force, but those who rely on Him that is stronger than all.

MR. HONEST AND MR. FEARING

I feared that you had been of the company of those that some time ago did rob Little-faith of his money; but now I look better about me, I perceive you are honester people.—The allegory requires us to suppose, that there were some places in which the Pilgrims might safely sleep; so that nothing disadvantageous to the character of this old disciple seems to have been intended. An avowed dependence on Christ for righteousness, a regard to the word of God, and an apparent sincerity in word and deed, mark a man to be a Pilgrim, or constitute a professor of the gospel: but we should not too readily conclude every professor to be a true believer. The experienced Christian will be afraid of new acquaintance; in his most unwatchful seasons he will be readily excited to look about him; and will be fully convinced that no enemy can hurt him, unless he is induced to yield to temptation and commit sin.

But, sir, said the old gentleman, how could you guess that I am such a man, since I came from such a place?—*Honesty in the abstract* seems to mean sinless perfection. The Pilgrim was a sound character, but conscious of many imperfections, of which he was ashamed, and from which he sought deliverance. The nature of faith, hope, love, patience, and other holy dispositions is described in Scripture, as a man would define gold, by its essential properties. This shows what they are *in the abstract:* but as exercised by us, they are always mixed with considerable alloy; and we are richer or poorer in this respect, in proportion to the degree of the gold or of the alloy which is found in our characters.

If the Sun of Righteousness will arise upon him, his frozen heart shall feel a thaw. And thus it hath been with me.—The Lord sometimes calls those sinners, whose character, connections, and situation, seem to place them at the greatest distance from him: that the riches of his mercy and the power of his grace may be thus rendered the more conspicuous and illustrious.

For men of my calling are oftentimes intrusted with the conduct of such as he was.—The character and narrative of Fearing has been generally admired by experienced readers, as drawn and arranged with great judgment, and in a very affecting manner. Little-faith, mentioned in the First Part, was fainthearted and distrustful; and thus he contracted guilt, and lost his comfort: but Fearing dreaded sin, and coming short of heaven, more than all that flesh could do unto him. He was alarmed at the least appearance or report of opposition; but this arose more from conscious weakness, and the fear of being overcome by temptation, than from a reluctance to undergo derision or persecution. The peculiarity of this description of Christians must be traced back to constitution, habit, first impressions, disproportionate and partial views of truth, and improper instructions; these concurring with weakness of faith, and the common infirmities of human nature, give a cast to their experience and character, which renders them uncomfortable to themselves, and troublesome to others. Yet no competent judges doubt but they have the root of the matter in them; and none are more entitled to the patient, sympathizing, and tender attention of ministers and Christians.

He loved to be in those two houses from which he came last, to wit, at the Gate, and that of the Interpreter, but that he durst not be so bold as to ask.—Christians, who resemble Fearing, are greatly retarded in their progress by discouraging apprehensions; they are apt to spend too much time in unavailing complaints; they do not duly profit by the counsel and assistance of their brethren; and they often neglect the proper means of getting relief from their terrors: yet they cannot think of giving up their feeble hopes, or of returning to their forsaken worldly pursuits and pleasures. They are, indeed, helped forward, through the mercy of God, in a very extraordinary manner: yet they still remain exposed to alarms and discouragements, in every stage of their pilgrimage: nor can they ever habitually rise superior to them. They are afraid even of relying on Christ for salvation; because they have not distinct views of his love, and the methods of his grace; and imagine some other qualification to be necessary, besides the willingness to seek, knock, and ask for the promised blessings, with a real desire of obtaining them. They imagine, that there has been something in their past life, or that there is some peculiarity in their present habits and propensities, and way of applying to Christ, which may exclude them from the general benefit: so that they pray with diffidence; and being consciously unworthy, can hardly believe that the Lord regards them, or will grant their requests. They are also prone to overlook the most decisive evidences of their reconciliation to God; and to persevere in arguing with perverse ingenuity against their own manifest happiness. The same mixture of humility and unbelief renders persons of this description backward in associating with their brethren, and in frequenting those companies in which they might obtain further instruction: for they are afraid of being considered as believers, or even serious inquirers; so that affectionate and earnest persuasion is requisite to prevail with them to join in those religious exercises by which Christians especially receive the teaching of the Holy Spirit. Yet this arises not from disinclination, but diffidence; and though they are often peculiarly favored with seasons of great comfort, to counterbalance their dejections; yet they never hear or read of those who 'have drawn back to perdition,' but they are terrified with the idea, that they shall shortly resemble them: so that every warning given against hypocrisy and self-deception seems to point them out by name, and every new discovery of any fault or mistake in their views, temper, or conduct, seems to decide their doom. At the same time, they are often remarkably melted into humble, admiring gratitude, by contemplating the love and sufferings of Christ, and seem to delight in hearing of that subject above all others. They do not peculiarly fear difficulties, self-denial, reproaches or persecution, which deter numbers from making an open profession of religion: and yet they are more backward in this respect than others; because they deem themselves unworthy to be admitted to such privileges, and into such society; or else are apprehensive of being finally separated from them, or becoming a disgrace to religion.

I suppose those enemies here had now a special check

*from our Lord, and a command not to meddle until Mr.
Fearing had passed over it.*—A low and obscure situation
suits the disposition of the persons here described: they do
not object to the most humiliating views of their own hearts,
of human nature, or of the way of salvation; they are little
tempted to covet eminence among their brethren, and find it
easier 'to esteem others better than themselves,' than persons
of a different frame of mind can well conceive. On the other
hand, their imaginations are peculiarly susceptible of impressions, and of the temptations represented by the valley of the
Shadow of Death: so that in this respect they need more than
others the tender and patient instructions of faithful ministers: while they repeat the same complaints, and urge the same
objections against themselves, that have already been obviated again and again. But the tender compassion of the Lord to
them should suggest an useful instruction to his servants, on
this part of their work.

*And didst thou fear the lake and pit? Would others
did so too! For, as for them that want thy wit, They do
themselves undo.*—No Christians are more careless about the
opinion of the world, or more zealous against its vanities, or
more watchful in times of ease and prosperity, than persons
of this description: but the prospect of death is often a terror
to them; especially when they suppose it to be at hand; yet
they often die with remarkable composure and comfort. Few
ministers, who have had an opportunity of carefully observing
the people intrusted to their pastoral care, can help thinking
of some individual, who might seem to have been the original
of this admirable portrait; which is full of instruction both to
them, and the timid, but conscientious part of their congregations. Indeed numbers, who are not characteristically Fearfuls,
have something of the same disposition in many particulars.
But such as fear reproach and self-denial more than those
things which this good man dreaded, bear a contrary character,
and are travelling the road to an opposite place: and even they
whose confidence of an interest in Christ far exceeds the degree
of their humiliation, conscientiousness, abhorrence of sin, and
victory over the world, may justly be suspected of having begun
their religion in a wrong manner; as they more resemble the
stony-ground hearers, who 'receive the word with joy, but have
no root in themselves,' than those who 'sow in tears, to reap in

joy.' For 'godly sorrow worketh repentance unto salvation, not to be repented of.'

Honesty: *There are many of this man's mind, that have not this man's mouth.*—The author peculiarly excels in contrasting his characters, of which a striking instance here occurs. The preceding episode relates to a very conscientious Christian, who, through weak faith and misapprehension, carried his self-suspicion to a troublesome and injurious extreme: and we have next introduced a false professor, who, pretending to strong faith, made his own obstinate self-will the only rule of his conduct. Yet in reality this arises from total unbelief: for the word of God declares such persons to be unregenerate, under the wrath of God, 'in the gall of bitterness and the bond of iniquity.' It would hardly be imagined, that men could be found maintaining such detestable sentiments as are here stated, did not facts most awfully prove it! We need not, however, spend time in exposing such a character: a general expression of the deepest detestation may suffice; for none who have been given up to such strong delusion, can reasonably be supposed accessible to the words of truth and soberness. Nor can they succeed in perverting others to such palpable and gross absurdities and abominable tenets; except they meet with those, that have long provoked God, by endeavoring to reconcile a wicked life with the hope of salvation. But it may properly be observed, that several expressions, which seem to represent *faith as an assurance of a personal interest* in Christ; or to intimate, that believers have *nothing to do with the law, even as the rule of their conduct;* with many unguarded assertions concerning the liberty of the gospel, and indiscriminate declamations against doubts, fears, and a legal spirit, have a direct tendency to prepare the mind of impenitent sinners, to receive the poisonous principles of avowed Antinomians. Much harm has been done in this way, and great disgrace brought upon the gospel: for there are many of this man's mind, who have not this man's mouth.

PART II · CHAPTER VIII

THE GUESTS OF GAIUS

Gaius: Yes, gentlemen, if you be true men, for my house is for none but pilgrims.—The spiritual refreshment arising from experimental and affectionate conversation with Christian friends, seems to be here more especially intended: yet the name of Gaius suggests also the importance of the apostle's exhortation, 'Use hospitality without grudging.' This ought to be attended to, even in respect of those with whom we have hitherto had no acquaintance, provided their characters are properly certified to us: for we are all brethren in Christ.

So this match was concluded, and in process of time they were married: but more of that hereafter.—The author availed himself of the opportunity, here presented him, of giving his opinion on a very important subject, about which religious persons often hold different sentiments. He evidently intended to say, that he deemed it generally most safe and advantageous to the parties themselves, and most conducive to the spread and permanency of true religion, for young Christians to marry; provided it be done in the fear of God, and according to the rules of his word. Yet we cannot suppose but he would readily have allowed of exceptions to this rule: for there are individuals, who, continuing single, employ that time and those talents in assiduously doing good, which in the married state must have been greatly abridged or preoccupied; and thus they are more extensively useful than their brethren. Yet, in common cases, the training up of a family, by the combined efforts of pious parents, in honesty, sobriety, industry, and the principles of true religion, when united with fervent prayer, and the persuasive eloquence of a good example, is so important a service to the church and to the community, that few persons are capable of doing greater or more permanent good in any other way. But this requires strict attention to the rules of scripture, in every step of these grand concerns: for children, brought up in ungodliness and ignorance, among those who are strangers to the gospel, are far more hopeful, than such as have received a bad education, witnessed bad examples, and imbibed worldly principles, in the families of evangelical professors.

Ope then the shells, and you shall have the meat; They here are brought for you to crack and eat.—The different parts of social worship and Christian fellowship are here allegorically described. The *heave-shoulder* and *wave-breast* prescribed in the ceremonial law, seem to have typified the power and love of our great High Priest; and to have conveyed an instruction to the priests to do their work with all their might, and with their whole heart: but they are here supposed to be also emblems of fervent prayer and grateful praise. The *wine* represents the exhilarating remembrance of the love of Christ in shedding his blood for us, and the application of the blessing to ourselves by living faith. The *milk* is the emblem of the plain, simple, and important instructions of Scripture, as brought forward by believers, when they meet together, for their edification. The *butter* and *honey* may denote those animating views of God, and realizing anticipations of heavenly joy, which tend greatly to establish the judgment, instruct the understanding, and determine the affections in cleaving to the good part that the believer hath chosen. The *apples* represent the promises and privileges, which believers possess by communion with Christ, in his ordinances; (Song of Solomon 2:3,) and the *nuts* signify such difficult subjects as experience and observation enable mature Christians to understand; and which amply repay the pains of endeavoring to penetrate their meaning, though they are not proper for the discussion of young converts. Whatever unbelievers may think, a company of Christians, employing themselves in the manner here described, have far sweeter enjoyments than they ever experienced when engaged in the mirth, diversions, and pleasures of the world: for these are merely the shadow of joy, but religion puts us in possession of the substance.

Mercy, as her custom was, would be making coats and garments to give to the poor, by which she brought a very good report upon pilgrims.—If our love to sinners be only shown by seeking their spiritual good, it will be considered as a mere bigoted desire to proselyte them to our sect or party: but uniform, diligent, and expensive endeavors to relieve their temporal wants are intelligible to every man, and bring a good report on the profession of the gospel.

If sin is Satan's cords, by which the soul lies bound, how should it make resistance before it is loosed from that infirmity.—The gracious operations of the Holy Spirit are here meant. These overcome our natural pride, love of sin, and aversion from God and religion; and then we repent, believe in Christ, are justified by faith, mortify sin, die to ourselves, and live to God in righteousness and true holiness.

The young one has the advantage of the fairest discovery of a work of grace within him, though the old man's corruptions are naturally the weakest.—Old age affords great advantages in overcoming some corrupt propensities: yet habits of indulgence often more than counterbalance the decays of nature; and avarice, suspicion, and peevishness, with other evils, gather strength as men advance in years. It is therefore in some particulars only, that age has the advantage over youth; and as some old men imagine that they have renounced sin, because they are no longer capable of committing the crimes in which they once lived, so there are young men, who presume that they shall live to be old, and imagine that repentance will then be comparatively easy to them: whereas sin, in one form or other, gathers strength and establishes its dominion, as long as it is permitted to reign in the soul. The instruction, however, that is here conveyed, is very important, provided it be properly understood; for if we do not estimate the advantages of our situation, we cannot determine how far external amendment results from internal renovation. During tedious diseases, or in the immediate prospect of death, men often feel very indifferent to the world, set against sin, disinclined to former indulgences, and earnest about salvation: yet returning health, business, company, and temptation, terminate such promising appearances. Many suppose themselves to be very good tempered, while every one studies to oblige them; yet provocation excites vehement anger and resentment in the breast: nay, riches and honor, while at a great distance, seem to have no charms for those, who are powerfully attracted by their magnetical influence, when placed within their reach!

When they were come home, they showed his head to the family, and set it up, as they had done others before, for a terror to those that should attempt to do as he hereafter.—The refreshment of divine consolations, and Christian fellowship, is intended to prepare us for vigorously maintaining the good fight of faith, not only against the enemies of our own souls, but also against the opposers of our holy religion, according to the talents intrusted to us, and the duties of our several stations. We are soldiers belonging to one great army under the command of the Captain of our salvation; and we ought to strive against sin, and 'contend for the faith once delivered to the saints,' by our profession, example, prayers, converse, and every other method authorized by the word of God. All that love the Lord are our brethren; and every thing that can mislead, dismay, or hinder any of them, should be considered as an adversary to the common cause; and we should counteract with meekness, but with firmness and decision, all the endeavors of those, who obstruct men in the ways of the Lord, or turn them aside into by-paths. It does not, however, clearly appear what particular description of opposers were represented by Slay-good: whether the author had in view certain selfish and malignant persecutors, who intimidated professors by fines and imprisonment, to the hazard of their lives, or of their souls; or some plausible heretics, who 'taught things which they ought not, for filthy lucre's sake,' to the total ruin of many that seemed hopeful, and the great detriment of others who were weak in faith and unestablished in judgment. The conflict seems merely to denote the efforts which Christians should make to prevent the effect of such opposition and delusion, and to remove such occasions of mischief out of the way; as also to show that the strong in faith are peculiarly called to these services, and ought not to shrink from hardship, danger, and suffering, in so good a cause.

I thank Him that loved me, I am fixed; my way is before me, my mind is beyond the river that has no bridge, though I am, as you see, but of a feeble mind.—The character of Feeble-mind seems to coincide in some things with that of Fearing; and in others with the description of Little-faith.

Constitutional timidity and lowness of spirits, arising from a feeble frame and frequent sickness, while they are frequently the means of exciting men to religion, give also a peculiar cast to their views and the nature of their profession; tend to hold them under perpetual discouragements, and unfit them for hard and perilous services. This seems implied in the name given to the native place of Feeble-mind: his *uncertainty* or hesitation in his religious profession was the effect of his natural turn of mind, which was opposite to the sanguine and confident. Yet this timid and discouraged irresolution is often connected with evident sincerity and remarkable perseverance in the ways of God. The principal difference between Feeble-mind and Fearing seems to be this: that the former was more afraid of opposition, and the latter more doubtful about the event; which perhaps may intimate, that Slay-good rather represents persecutors than deceivers.

He was also with me when Slay-good the giant took me, but he was nimble of his heels, and escaped: but it seems he escaped to die, and I was taken to live.—Here again we meet with a contrast between a feeble believer and a specious hypocrite. The latter eludes persecution by time-serving, yet perishes in his sins: the former suffers and trembles, yet hopes; is delivered and comforted, and finds his trials terminate in his greater advantage. The frequency with which this difference is introduced, and the variety of character by which it is illustrated, shows us how important the author deemed it, to warn false professors at the same time that we comfort the feebleminded, and to mark as exactly as we can the discriminating peculiarities of their aim and experience.

We will not enter into doubtful disputations before you; we will be made all things to you, rather than you shall be left behind.—Weak believers are conscientious even to scrupulosity: so far from allowing themselves in the practice of known sin, or the omission of evident duty, they are prone to abridge themselves in things which are indifferent; they often impose rules on themselves which they do not expect others to observe; and sometimes are sensible that their uneasiness, at the liberty used by their brethren, arises from ignorance and low attainments: and therefore they deem it better to live retired, than to burden others with their peculiarities, or be grieved with things which every where meet their observation.

But there are persons, that expect to be encouraged as weak believers, who are far removed from such scrupulousness; and whose weakness consists merely in an inability to maintain an unwavering confidence, while they live in a loose and negligent manner. These seem more to resemble Not-right than Feeble-mind. They that are indeed weak believers, should learn from this passage, to beware of censoriousness, and of making themselves a standard for others: and their stronger brethren should be reminded not to despise or grieve them, by an inexpedient use of their liberty. (The author, in a marginal note, has marked Great-heart's answer as a *Christian spirit*.) They will, however, commonly find associates, in some measure of their own turn, who are often more useful to them, than such as cannot entirely sympathize with their feelings.

Honesty: Say you so? I dare say it was a hard chapter that then he did read unto them.—The near prospect of persecution is formidable even to true believers, notwithstanding all the encouragements of God's word. It is therefore very useful to realize such scenes to our minds, and to consider how we should feel were they actually present; that we may be preserved from self-confidence; excited to diligence in every thing connected with the assurance of hope; put on our guard against every action or engagement which might weaken our confidence in God; and pray without ceasing, for that measure of wisdom, fortitude, patience, meekness, faith and love, which might be sufficient for us, should matters come to the worst.

PART II - CHAPTER IX

VANITY FAIR AND MR. MNASON'S HOUSE

The sight of good men to them that are going on pilgrimage, is like to the appearing of the moon and stars to them that are sailing upon the seas.—Even in those populous cities, where vanity most prevails, and where persecution at some seasons has most raged, a remnant of real Christians generally reside; and believers will in every place inquire after such persons and associate with them. (Psalm 119:63; 1 John 3:14.)

True, there were some of the baser sort, that could see no more than a mole, nor understand any more than a beast; these had no reverence for these men, nor took they notice of their valor and adventures.—This seems to refer to the prevalence of popery for some time before the revolution in 1688; by which many nominal protestants were drawn aside, and numbers of children educated in the principles of that dark superstition. The favor or frown of the Prince and his party operated so powerfully, that worldly men in general yielded to the imposition: but several persons among the nonconformists, as well as the established church, did eminent service at that crisis by their preaching and writings, in exposing the delusions and abominations of that monstrous religion; and these endeavors were eventually the means of overturning the plan formed for the re-establishment of popery in Britain. The disinterested and bold decided conduct of many dissenters, on this occasion, procured considerable favor, both to them and their brethren, with the best friends of the nation: but the prejudices of others prevented them from reaping *all* the advantage from it that they ought to have done.

PART II · CHAPTER X

DELECTABLE MOUNTAINS AND THE SHEPHERDS

Besides, here they shall be sure to have good nurture and admonition, and shall be taught to walk in right paths, and that you know is a favor of no small account.—Under this emblem we are taught the importance of early recommending our children to the faithful care of the Lord Jesus, by fervent prayer, with earnest desires of their eternal good, above all secular advantages whatsoever; consequently we ought to keep them at a distance from such places, connections, books, and companies, as may corrupt their principles and morals; to instill such pious instructions as they are capable of receiving; to bring them early under the preaching of the gospel and to the ordinances of God; and to avail ourselves of every help, in thus 'training them up in the nurture and admonition of the Lord.' For depraved natural propensities, the course of the world, the artifices of Satan, the inexperience, credulity, and sanguine expectations of youth, the importance of the case, and the precepts of Scripture, concur in requiring this conduct of us. Yet, after all, our minds must be anxious about the event, in proportion as we value their souls, except as we find relief, by commending them to the faithful care of that tender Shepherd, who 'gathers the lambs with his arm, and carries them in his bosom.'

Set it upon a pole by the highway-side, right over against the pillar that Christian erected for a caution to pilgrims, that came after, to take heed of entering into his grounds.—The following lines are here added, as in other places:—

'Though Doubting-Castle be demolished,
And Giant Despair too has lost his head;
Sin can rebuild the Castle, make 't remain
And make Despair the Giant live again.'—

Indeed they seem to be much wanted; for the exploit of destroy-
ing Doubting-Castle, and killing Giant Despair, is more liable
to exception than any incident in the whole work. To relieve
the minds of such as are discouraged in the path of duty, or
when inquiring the way of salvation, is doubtless a most important service in the cause of Christ. This is represented by the
attempts made to mend the road over the Slough of Despond; but
By-path Meadow ought to lead to Doubting-Castle; such inward
distresses are as useful to Christians as any other rebukes and
corrections, by which their loving Friend renders them watchful and circumspect. Could this order be reversed, it would give
strength to temptation, and tend to embolden men to seek relief
from difficulties by transgression; for the apprehension of subsequent distress is one grand preventive, even to the believer,
when such measures are suggested to his mind. Indeed this is
the Lord's method of performing his covenant to his people; 'I
will,' says he, 'put my fear in their hearts, that they shall not
depart from me.' (Jeremiah 32:40.) If therefore *love* be not in
lively exercise, he has so ordered it, that *fear* should intervene,
to prevent worse consequences. So that, when believers have
not only departed from the way, but have also fallen asleep on
forbidden ground, their alarms and doubts are salutary, though
often groundless and extreme; and should any man, by preaching or writing, be able to prevent all the despondings of such
persons, previous to their repentance and its happy effects, he
would subserve the design of the tempter, and counteract the
Lord's plan. We can, with propriety, do no more in this case,
than encourage the fallen to repent and seek forgiveness, by
the general truths, invitations, and promises of Scripture; and
comfort them, when penitent, by suitable topics, 'that they may
not be swallowed up of overmuch sorrow.' But though this part
of the allegory is liable to some objection, or capable of being
abused; yet it is probable, that the author only intended to
show, that the labors of faithful ministers, with the converse
and prayers of such believers as are strong in faith, may be
very useful in recovering the fallen, and relieving them that are
ready to despond; and of thus preventing the more durable and

dreadful effects of the weak believer's transgressions.

Then said Mr. Great-heart, I know him, he is a man above many.—Faith, exercised on the promises, and according to the warrant of Scripture, engages the arm of Omnipotence on our side, as far as our duty or advantage, and the glory of God are concerned: so that strong faith will remove out of our way, every obstacle which prevents our progress. But many things seem to us to be insurmountable obstacles which are merely trials of our patience, or 'thorns in the flesh' to keep us humble; no degree of faith therefore will remove them; but believing prayer will be answered by inward strength communicated to our souls. 'The grace of the Lord Jesus will be sufficient for us:' 'his strength will be perfected in our weakness:' the burning bush shall not be consumed: and we shall be enabled to proceed, though in great weakness and with many trembling apprehensions. On the other hand, real hindrances frequently obstruct our path, 'because of our unbelief,' and because we neglect the proper means of increasing our faith. (Matthew 17:19–21.)

For God, by that a little time is spent, will cause that their innocence shall break forth as the light, and their righteousness as the noonday.—This and the subsequent emblems are sufficiently *explained,* and only require to be duly *considered* with reference to their practical import. It may, however, be observed, that some godly men have been suspected of crimes charged upon them by prejudiced persons, of which they are entirely innocent: yet, perhaps, this will be found to have originated from some misconduct in other respects, or from want of circumspection in 'avoiding the appearance of evil:' so that the general rule may be allowed to be valid; and they who feel themselves to be exceptions to it will do well to examine whether they have not, by indiscretion, at least, exposed themselves to this painful trial. I apprehend most of us have cause enough in this respect for humiliation and patience.

So, Sincere ran and fetched it, and with a joyful consent it was given her. Then she bowed her head, and gave thanks, and said, By this I know that I have obtained favor in your eyes.—The Holy Scriptures, revealing to us the mysteries and perfections of God, showing us our own real character and condition, and discovering Christ and his salvation to our souls, are represented under this emblem. Every true believer longs to be more completely acquainted with them from day to day, and to look into them continually.

Wherefore, here was the advantage that this company had over the other.—The author embraces every opportunity of pointing out the important advantages of the pastoral office, when faithfully executed; by which he meant the regular care of a stated minister over a company of professed Christians who are his peculiar charge, have voluntarily placed themselves under his instructions, seek counsel from him in all their difficulties, and pay regard to his private admonitions; being convinced that he uprightly seeks their spiritual welfare, and is capable of promoting it. Nothing so much tends to the establishment and consistent conduct of believers, or the *permanent* success of the gospel, as a proper reciprocal attention of pastors and their flocks to each other. A general way of preaching and hearing, with little or no connection, cordial, unreserved intercourse, or even acquaintance, between ministers and their congregations; with continual changes from one place to another, may tend to spread a superficial knowledge of evangelical truth more widely: but, through the want of seasonable reproof, counsel, encouragement, or admonition, the general directions delivered from the pulpit will seldom be recollected when they are most wanted. Hence it is, that professors so often miss their way, are taken in the Flatterer's net, and fall asleep on the Enchanted Ground: and a faithful guide, ever at hand, to give the caution or direction at the time, is the proper remedy, for which no adequate substitute can be found. But, as it is much easier to preach at large on general topics, and, after a few sermons delivered in one congregation, to go over the same ground again in another place; than to perform duly the several parts of the arduous office, which is sustained by the stated pastor of a regular congregation: and as it is far more agreeable to nature, to be exempted from private admonitions, than to be troubled with them, it may be feared, that this important subject will not at present be duly attended to.

PART II · CHAPTER XI

MR. VALIANT FOR TRUTH

Hear your horse dash, and so they betook themselves to flight.—From the names given to the opponent, with whom the Pilgrim fought, we may infer, that the author meant to represent by them certain *wild* enthusiasts, who, not having ever duly considered any religious subject, officiously intrude themselves in the way of professors; to perplex their minds, and persuade them, that unless they adopt their reveries or superstitions, they cannot be saved. An ungovernable imagination, a mind incapable of sober reflection, and a dogmatizing spirit, characterize these enemies of the truth: they assault religious persons with specious reasonings, cavilling objections, confident assertions, bitter reproaches, proud boastings, sarcastical censures, and rash judgments: they endeavor to draw them over to their party, or to drive them from attending to religion at all; or to terrify them with the fears of damnation, in their present endeavors to serve God, and find his salvation. Whatever company of persons we suppose that the author had in view, we may learn from the passage, what our strength, hope, and conduct ought to be, when we are thus assaulted. The word of God, used in faith, and with fervent and persevering prayer, will enable us at length to silence such dangerous assailants: and if we be *valiant for the truth*, and meekly contend for it, amidst revilings, menaces, and contempt, we may hope to confirm others also, and to promote the common cause.

Valiant: They said it was an idle life.—This hath been the reproach cast on religion in every age. Pharaoh said to Moses and the Israelites, 'Ye are idle, ye are idle; therefore ye say, let us go and do sacrifice to the Lord.' Men naturally imagine, that time spent in the immediate service of God is wasted: should a Christian therefore employ as many hours every week, in reading the Scriptures, in secret and social prayer, in pious discourse, and in attending on public ordinances, as his neighbor devotes to amusement and sensual indulgence; an outcry would speedily be made, about his idling away his time, and being in the way to beggar his family! As this must be expected, it behoves all believers to avoid every appearance of evil, and by exemplary diligence in their proper employments, a careful redemption of time, a prudent frugality in their expenses, and a good management of all their affairs, to 'put to silence the ignorance of foolish men.' For there are too many favorers of the gospel, who give plausibility to these slanders, by running from place to place, that they may hear every new preacher; while the duties of the family, and of their station in the community are miserably neglected. They 'walk disorderly, working not at all, but are busybodies:' from these we ought to withdraw, and against such professors we should protest: for they are 'ever learning, but never able to come to the knowledge of the truth.'

But not one of them had found so much advantage by going as amounted to the weight of a feather.—Worldly people, in opposing the gospel, descant abundantly on the folly and hypocrisy of religious persons; they pick up every vague report that they hear to their disadvantage, and narrowly watch for the halting of such as they are acquainted with; and then they form general conclusions, from a few particular, distorted, and uncertain stories! Thus they endeavor to prove, that there is no reality in religion, that it is impossible to find the way to heaven, and that it is better to be quiet than to bestow pains to no purpose. This frivolous sophistry is frequently employed, after all other arguments have been silenced. But it is vain to deny the existence of hypocrites and deceivers; or to excuse the evils to which they object: on the contrary, we should allow these representations, as far as there is any appearance of truth in them; and then show that this teaches us to beware lest we be deceived, and to try every doctrine by the touchstone of God's word; that counterfeits prove the value of the thing counterfeited; that we should learn to distinguish between the precious and the vile; and, finally, that while danger may attend a religious profession, irreligion insures destruction.

PART II · CHAPTER XII

THE ENCHANTED GROUND

This arbor was called The Slothful's Friend, on purpose to allure, if it might be, some of the pilgrims there to take up their rest when weary.—This view of the Enchanted Ground seems to vary from that which has been considered in the First Part. The circumstances of believers who are deeply engaged in business, and constrained to spend much time among worldly people, may here be particularly intended. This may sometimes be unavoidable; but it is *enchanted ground:* many professors, fascinated by the advantages and connections thus presented to them, fall asleep, and wake no more: and others are entangled by those thorns and briers, which 'choke the word, and render it unfruitful.' The more soothing the scene the greater the danger, and the more urgent need is there for watchfulness and circumspection: the more vigilant believers are, the greater uneasiness will such scenes occasion them; as they will be so long out of their proper element: and the weaker and more unestablished men are, the more apt will they be, in such circumstances, to yield to discouragement. The society and counsel of faithful ministers and Christian friends may help them to get on: but they will often feel that their path is miry and slippery, entangling and perplexing, dark and wearisome to their souls. Yet if this be the case, their sighs, complaints, and prayers, are hopeful symptoms: but when worldly employments and connections, which perhaps at first were in a sense unavoidable, induce prosperity, and men seek comfort from this prosperity, instead of considering it as a snare or burden, or improving it as a talent; then the professor falls asleep in the enchanted arbor. It behoves, however, all who love their souls, to shun that hurry of business, and multiplicity of affairs and projects, into which many are betrayed by degrees, in order to supply increasing expenses, that might be avoided by strict frugality and more moderate desires: for these things lade the soul with thick clay; are a heavy weight to the most upright; render a man's way doubtful and joyless; and 'drown many in destruction and perdition.'

Then thought I with myself, Who that goeth on pilgrimage but would have one of these maps about him, that he may look when he is at a stand which is the way he must take?—This emblem inculcates the duty of constant attention to the *precepts* and *counsels* of Scripture, as well as reliance on its *promises;* and of an habitual application to the Lord by prayer, to teach us the true meaning of his word, that we may learn the way of peace and safety, in the most difficult and doubtful cases; and the advantage of consulting such ministers, as are most experienced in the ways of God, and most conversant with his sacred oracles.

Wherefore let pilgrims look to themselves, lest it happen to them as it has done to these that, as you see, are fallen asleep, and none can awake them.—Such men as take up a profession of the gospel, in a heedless manner, and proceed with an overbearing confidence, the result of pride and ignorance, may long maintain a form of godliness, though it be a weariness to them: but after a time they will gradually be drawn back into the world, retaining nothing of their religion, except certain distorted doctrinal notions. They find excuses for their conduct from false maxims, and bad examples; they fall asleep in the arms of worldly prosperity; nothing can awaken them to fear, or self-suspicion; but they will, as it were, talk in their sleep about religion, in so incoherent a manner, as to excite the laughter of children; while they who understand the case will bewail their deplorable delusion. Such awful examples should excite us to redoubled diligence, in searching the Scriptures, and in prayer; lest we too should be overcome with a destructive sleep, and perish in this fascinating way. For scenes of worldly prosperity have detected the hypocrisy of many, who have long persevered in an unsuspected profession, amidst difficulties and trials.

Then I betook me, as you saw, to my knees, and with

hands lifted up, and cries, I prayed to Him, that had said he would help.—The case of Standfast shows us, that when believers feel the propensity of their hearts to yield to worldly proposals, it renders them jealous of themselves, excites them to earnest prayer, and thus eventually tends to preserve them from the fatal delusions.

PART II · CHAPTER XIII

THE PILGRIMS AT HOME

Only when they tasted of the water of the river over which they were to go, they thought that it tasted a little bitterish to the palate; but it proved sweet when it was down.—The lively exercise of faith and hope, the anticipation of heavenly felicity, and the consolations of the Holy Spirit, soon make the believer forget his conflicts and sorrows, or only remember them to enhance his grateful joy. This description represents the happy state of those that live in places, favored with many lively Christians, united in heart and judgment; and where instances of persons dying triumphantly are often reported or witnessed. It has frequently been observed, that aged believers, in such circumstances, have been remarkably delivered from fears and temptations, and animated by the hopes and earnests of heaven; so that while death seemed bitter to nature, it became pleasant to the soul, to think of the joy and glory that would immediately follow it.

The token was, an arrow with a point sharpened with love, led easily into her heart, which by degrees wrought so effectually with her, that at the time appointed she must be gone.—These messengers seem to be merely emblems of the different diseases or decays, by which the Lord takes down the earthly tabernacle, when he sees good to receive the souls of his people into his immediate presence. In plain language, it was reported that Christiana was sick and near death, and she herself became sensible of her situation. 'The arrow sharpened by love,' implies, that the time, manner, and circumstances of the believer's death are appointed by Him 'who loved us, and gave himself for us:' He, as it were, says to the dying saint, 'It is I, be not afraid.'

Only I advise thee to repent of thine aptness to fear and doubt of his goodness, before he sends for thee; lest thou shouldst, when he comes, be forced to stand before him for that fault with blushing.—The address made by Christiana to each of the company, and the circumstances of her passing the river, are well deserving of attention; but require no comment. When such believers as have long walked honorably, are enabled to bear a dying testimony to the truth, and to recommend the ways of the Lord with the last remains of their breath, a great effect will often be produced: but the confidence of some professors, in these circumstances, has a very different tendency. Many excellent persons, however, are incapacitated from speaking much in their last hours; and we ought by no means to judge of men's characters on these grounds: for it is remarkable, that the Scripture is generally silent about the *manner* in which its worthies terminated their lives; and a very few exceptions are found to this rule. We are particularly instructed in the nature of their faith, and its effects upon their conduct during life; and thence we may assuredly infer, that they died in the Lord, and entered into rest.

At her departure, the children wept. But Mr. Greatheart and Mr. Valiant played upon the well-tuned cymbal and harp for joy. So all departed to their respective places.—The happy death of an eminent Christian is a loss to relatives and connections, to the church and the community; and in this view may be lamented: but it often yields great encouragement to ministers and other spectators of the interesting scene, and excites their adoring praise and thanksgivings.

My message is to tell thee that he expects thee at his table to sup with him in his kingdom, the next day after Easter; wherefore prepare thyself for this journey.— Evident decays of natural powers as effectually convince the observing person that death approaches, as if a messenger had been sent to inform him. But men in general cling to life, wilfully overlook such tokens, and try to keep up to the last the vain hope of recovering; and others, by a kind of cruel compassion, soothe them in the delusion: so that numbers die *suddenly* of *chronical* disorders, even as if they had been shot through the heart. Perhaps, however, the author had some reference to those inexplicable presages of death, which some persons evidently experience.

"I have broken thy golden bowl, and loosed thy silver cord."—These tokens are taken from a well-known portion of Scripture; but it would be inconsistent with the plan of this work, to enter on a particular explanation of them. The dealings of the Lord are here represented, as uniformly gentle to the feeble, trembling, humble believers; and the circumstances of their deaths comparatively encouraging and easy.

He hath held me, and hath kept me from mine iniquities; yea, my steps hath he strengthened in his way.— This speech has been justly admired, as one of the most striking passages in the whole work: but it is so plain, that it only requires an attentive reader. It may, however, be worthy of our observation, that in all the instances before us the Pilgrims are represented as resting their only dependence, at the closing scene, on the mercy of God, through the righteousness and atonement of his Son: and yet recollecting their conscious integrity, boldness in professing and contending for the truth, love to the cause, example, and words of Christ, obedience to his precepts, delight in his ways, preservation from their own iniquities, and consistent behavior, as evidences that their faith was living, and their hope warranted; and in this way the retrospect conduced to their encouragement. Moreover, they all concur in declaring, that while they left their infirmities behind them, they should take their graces along with them, and that 'their works would follow them.' Thus the scriptural mean is exactly maintained, between those who place their *supposed* good works as the *foundation* of their hope; and those, who would exclude even *real* good works from being so much as looked upon, as *evidential* of saving faith, or as in any way giving encouragement to the believer in his dying hour.

With trumpeters and pipers, with singers and players upon stringed instruments, to welcome the pilgrims as they went up, and followed one another in at the beautiful gate of the city.—The view given in this place, of the peaceful and joyful death of the Pilgrims, cannot but affect every reader in some degree; and many perhaps may be ready to say, 'Let me die the death of the righteous, and let my last end be like his:' but, except they make it their principal concern to live the life of the righteous, such a wish will most probably be frustrated;

and every hope grounded on it is evidently presumptuous, as the example of Balaam sufficiently proves. If any man, therefore, doubt whether this allegory do indeed describe the Rise and Progress of religion in the soul; the beginning, continuance, and termination of the godly man's course to heaven; let him diligently search the Scriptures, and fervently pray to God, from whom alone 'cometh every good and perfect gift,' to enable him to determine this question. But let such as own themselves to be satisfied that it does, beware lest they rest on this assent and notion, in the pleasure of reading an ingenious work on the subject, or in the ability of developing many of the author's emblems. Let them beware lest they be fascinated, as it were, into a persuasion, that they actually accompany the Pilgrims in the life of faith, and walking with God, in the same measure, as they keep pace with the author, in discovering and approving the grand outlines of his plan. And let every one carefully examine his state, sentiments, experience, motives, tempers, affections and conduct, by the various characters, incidents, and observations, that pass under his review; assured that this is a matter of the greatest consequence. We ought not indeed to call any man *master,* or subscribe absolutely to all his sentiments; yet the diligent *practical* student of Scripture can scarcely doubt, but that the warnings, counsels, and instructions of this singular work, agree in general with that sacred touchstone; or that characters and actions will at last be approved or condemned by the Judge of the world, in a great degree according to the sentence passed on them in this wise and faithful book. The Lord grant that the readers of these observations 'may find mercy in that day,' and be addressed in these gracious words, 'Come, ye blessed of my Father, inherit the kingdom prepared for you, from the foundation of the world.'

Printed in Great Britain
by Amazon